Handbook of Western Civilization:

Beginnings to 1700

HANDBOOK

OF WESTERN CIVILIZATION:

BEGINNINGS TO 1700

by Sidney A. Burrell

Barnard College, Columbia University

John Wiley & Sons, Inc., New York · London · Sydney

Portions of this book are revised and adapted from
ESSENTIALS OF WESTERN CIVILIZATION: THE MAIN STRANDS
OF DEVELOPMENT FROM THE BEGINNINGS TO THE
18TH CENTURY, © 1959 by Howard Chandler, Publisher.

Library of Congress Catalog Card Number: 65-17858
Printed in the United States of America

PREFACE

This Preface contains some useful study suggestions.
Be sure to read it before you go on with the book!

The intention of this book is to give you more than just an outline of historical facts. It also gives you a summary of the major movements and ideas in western civilization into which the facts can be fitted. By giving you this summary and framework it will help you to answer essay questions as well as factual and objective questions in examinations.

To make it easier for you to study, the chapters are divided into sections which make it possible for you to approach the understanding of western civilization one step at a time. If you will proceed with your reading in the following way, you should find it fairly easy to absorb the subject matter as you go along.

First: Read Chapter 1, *What Western Civilization Is.* It contains the main developments or themes stressed in this book. And also read Chapter 10, *The Western World in 1700.* It is a summation of what you will find in Chapters 2-9, and much that is in these chapters will make more sense to you as you read them if you have first read Chapters 1 and 10.

Next: Read Chapters 2-9. Notice that each of these chapters has two kinds of reading matter that cover the same historic topics but in different ways. The first kind (the Essential Movement) explains the main movements of a convenient chunk of history. The second kind (Events and Definitions) gives an outline of facts and additional explanatory material for the same chunk of history. If you read these parts in their order, you will avoid the problem of trying to absorb too much unfamiliar historical detail before you know what a chunk of history is all about. You can end with a firm and confident feel of the historical period.

Often: Check you memory for ideas and factual details by referring to the brief chronological chart that follows this page.

Finally: Read Chapter 10; and if you think it may help, read Chapter 1 again.

If you follow this plan carefully, step by step, you will
find that you have come to a clear idea of the development
of western civilization and to a sound grasp of factual details.

The Periods of History: Beginnings to 1700

Period of Time	Political Developments	Social Life and Urbanization	Science and Technology	Intellectual Developments
Paleolithic (Old Stone) Age. to c. 12,000 B.C.	Family, clan, or tribal organization.	Probably little or no village organization.	Age of food gathering. Tools made of bone, stone, or wood.	Little or no systematized thought; cave drawings.
Mesolithic (Middle Stone) Age. c. 12,000–c. 8000 B.C.	As above; probably some village organization.	Villages.	Dog domesticated; bow and arrow used.	Probably no systematized thought.
Neolithic (New Stone) Age c. 8000–5000 B.C. Major revolution in human development	Family, clan, tribe.	Villages.	First use of agriculture (food growing), domestic animals, polished tools. "Neolithic Revolution."	Probably no systematized thought; primitive art forms.
Chalcolithic (Copper and Stone) Age. c. 5000–c. 3500 B.C.	Family, clan, tribe; possibly primitive kingship.	Transition from village to city.	Period of transition when metalworking became common.	Probably no systematized thought.
Bronze Age. after c. 3500 B.C. Iron Age. after c. 1800 B.C.	Rise of city-states and territorial kingdoms: formation of Mesopotamian city-states; union of Upper and Lower Egypt, c. 3200.	Beginning of urban life ("Urban Revolution"), c. 3000; rise of commercial exchange; extension of communication.	Use of copper and tin to make bronze; introduction of iron marked last major step in development of metallurgy.	Formulation of mathematics; early astronomy; codes of law; religious rituals and ethics codified; writing developed.
The Ancient Empires to 600 B.C.	Evolution of the divine kingship of Pharaoh; formation	Large cities appear; commerce enlarged and extended.	Development of navigation and shipbuilding; applied	Evolution of highly developed religious systems: cult

Period	Political History	Economic and Social	Science	Religion and Philosophy
	of extended territorial empires (Akkadians, Cretans, Babylonians, Hittites, Assyrians, Egyptians). Persian Empire emerges (c. 600) as greatest united empire of the ancient world before Rome.		mathematics; early astronomical calculations.	of Ikhnaton in Egypt; Hebrew prophets; Zoroastrianism.
Hellenic Age. c. 600-300 B.C.	"Universal" empire of Persia extended its sway throughout the eastern Mediterranean; rise of the Greek city-state (*polis*). Persian Empire defeated by Greeks (490-479); conquered by Alexander the Great, 330.	Continued expansion of city and commercial life; great age of Athens under Pericles, 5th century.	Formulation of Pythagorean geometry. 6th century Greeks observe and speculate on the order of nature.	Greeks develop first true school of philosophy (Milesians), 6th century. Golden Age of philosophy, 5th and 4th centuries: Socrates, Plato, Aristotle.
Hellenistic Period. c. 300-30 B.C.	Universal empire of Alexander disintegrated into smaller despotic monarchies; Carthaginian Empire destroyed by the rising Roman Republic; expansion of Rome.	Growth of commerce and wealth; high level of urban civilization. End of the Greek city-states. Period of great material advance.	Great scientific and technological advances: Euclid (geometry), c. 300 B.C.; Archimedes (physics), 3rd century B.C.	Hellenic culture spread to all parts of Mediterranean world. Philosophy (Epicureanism, Stoicism, Skepticism) partially displaced religious belief.
Roman Empire. c. 30 B.C.-500 A.D.	Rome became Empire under Augustus, 23 B.C. Mediterranean world unified; Rome reached greatest territorial extent, 117 A.D. Empire Christianized under Constantine, 337. End of western Roman Empire, 476. Romans achieve high level of government organization and centralization.	Under Roman protection (*Pax Romana*) city life and commerce increased. Economic life of Mediterranean centered on Rome, which had a population of about one million at its height.	Romans reach a high level of practical engineering: road-building, ship construction, aqueducts. No great theoretical advances in science.	Hellenistic philosophies and eastern religious cults gradually superseded by Christianity. Christian theology formulated by the early fathers (Augustine, *et al.*) and partly fused with Greek philosophy.

Period of Time	Political Developments	Social Life and Urbanization	Science and Technology	Intellectual Developments
Early Medieval Europe. c. 500-1000 A.D.	Centralized Roman imperial government gave way to Germanic successor states. Localized feudal government supplanted Roman bureaucracy. Attempt to revive western empire under Charlemagne (800) failed.	Rise of manorialism; decline of city life in northern and western Europe.	Except in Byzantium and Arab world, knowledge was attenuated. Classical influences restricted to narrow elite.	Spread of Christianity; rise of monasticism in the West. Carolingian Renaissance, 8th century.
High Middle Ages. c. 1000-1400	Revival of the imperial idea: Holy Roman Empire founded, 10th century. Rise of medieval papacy: Gregory VII (1073-1085), Innocent III (1198-1216), Boniface VIII (1294-1303). Papal decline began with Great Schism, 1378-1417. Growth of feudal kingship marked beginning of national state. Crusading movements in Palestine (1099-1204), Spain, and the Baltic region.	Growth of medieval towns after 1000; increase in commerce and wealth; towns undermined feudal agrarian society.	Gradual improvement in agricultural techniques; growing commercial and productive specialization; beginning of large-scale textile manufacture in Flanders and Italy.	Renaissance of the 12th century; Anselm, Abelard; spread of Aristotle's writings through western Europe. Founding of Universities: Bologna, Paris, Oxford, Cambridge. Growth of scholasticism: St. Thomas Aquinas (1225-1274).
Renaissance and Reformation. c. 1400-1600	Appearance of new centralized monarchies; decline of feudal nobility; England, France, Spain emerged as strongest states of western Europe. Beginning of great discoveries: da Gama, Columbus, Magellan. Luther began Protestant revolt against medieval church, 1517. Spread of	Rich city civilizations in Italy and Flanders. New business techniques ("rise of the capitalist spirit") stimulated commerce. Appearance of commercial financiers: Medici, Fuggers. Price Revolution increases European cost of living.	Improvements in manufacture: first "industrial revolution," c. 1540-1640. Copernicus's *De Revolutionibus*, 1543. Improvements in navigation and shipbuilding.	Thinkers of the Renaissance (Petrarch, Machiavelli) reacted against scholasticism; growing interest in classical literature; shift in outlook from other worldliness to things of this world (humanism). Protestant leaders reject sacramental views of medieval church; stress faith against works.

	Political	Economic/Social	Scientific	Cultural/Philosophical
	Protestantism: Sweden (1527), England (1534), Denmark (1536), Geneva (under Calvin, 1540), Scotland (1560), Netherlands (revolt against Spain began, 1567). Counter-Reformation: founding of Jesuits, 1540; Council of Trent, 1545-1563. Emergence of Spain as leading European power, 1559.	Cities increase in size: London and Paris with $1/2$ million become largest in Europe. Commercial Revolution stimulates capital growth throughout Europe. High point of the mercantile system.	Scientific Revolution: change in man's outlook toward universe. Galileo (1564-1642); Newton (1642-1727).	Impact of the Scientific Revolution felt in philosophy; rise of rationalism. Age of the Baroque in art and architecture.
Age of Absolutism. c. 1600-1700	Development of strong monarchy in France: Richelieu, Mazarin, Louis XIV. Puritan Revolution in England (1642-1649); Glorious Revolution, 1688. Beginning of Prussian state under Great Elector, 1640-1688. Westernization of Russia by Peter the Great. Emergence of France as strongest state of western Europe, 1659.			
The Western World. 1700-1789 (Enlightenment and the Old Regime)	Divine Right theory of monarchy superseded by "enlightened despotism." Emergence of Prussia and Russia as major European powers. England became leading maritime power after Peace of Utrecht, 1713. Overseas expansion accelerated; Anglo-French colonial wars, 1689-1783. American Revolution, 1776-1783.	Steady rise in European population. Capital growth speeded industrialization in western Europe. Rising social criticism in France.	Newton's discoveries stimulated growth of theoretical science; laws of nature regarded as finally ascertainable by science. Major advances in chemistry, astronomy, biology. Increase in rate of invention (Watt's steam engine, etc.) after 1750.	Newtonian synthesis led to belief in mechanical universe: all knowledge explainable in terms of "natural law"; rise of the "social sciences"; influence of the French *philosophes*; enlightened individualism and theory of progress dominate philosophy.

CONTENTS

CHAPTER 1

What Western Civilization Is:
Its Components and Its Themes

THE ESSENTIAL MOVEMENT

When we speak of "western civilization," though there are a number of special and often technical definitions of the term, we tend to have in mind some such general definition as the following: Western civilization is that body of political, social, religious, and intellectual traditions developed by the peoples who have lived in historic time (about five thousand years) within the regions of the Mediterranean Basin, including the Near East, North Africa, the continent of Europe, and the latter's cultural offshoots in the western hemisphere, Australia, New Zealand, and South Africa. It is the inheritor of the ancient Mediterranean civilizations—Egyptian, Mesopotamian, Hebrew, Greek, and Roman—and has been most influenced in its religious development by Judaism and Christianity, though, at certain periods and somewhat less directly, it has also felt the influence of Islam (Mohammedanism).

Will this definition do? Let us consider four of many possible approaches to revising it.

First: In more recent times, because its centers of population and power have been located in Europe and North America, western civilization is often thought of, not always correctly, as a peculiar manifestation of the highly industrialized nations of the North Atlantic region.

Second: With the passage of time, the definable historic components

1

of western civilization have altered and changed. For example, with the rise of modern science and technology, the latter have come to be thought of as peculiar, definitive attributes of the western world, as they are to a very large extent. Science and technology were not, however, always the peculiar properties of the West, though western civilization had much to do with their creation in modern form.

Third: While many westerners now think of the culture of the Moslem world as something separate and distinct from that of the West, it must be remembered that before the appearance of the Prophet Mohammed in the 7th century A.D., many of the areas of the Near East and North Africa were part of the cultural complex out of which later western civilization developed; they were peopled by those who looked to Rome and to Constantinople.

Fourth: We must also bear in mind that one of the striking things about western civilization is that it has gradually expanded over many centuries until it is well on its way to becoming a worldwide civilization. That is not to say that Asian or African peoples are interested in adopting all the traditions of the western world. Many of these latter, including certain western religious beliefs and social practices, are rejected by nonwestern peoples. What most of these peoples want, however, are the technological and scientific skills that have given the western world a relatively higher scale of living than the rest of the world has possessed in modern times. Whether nonwestern societies can successfully adopt western science and technology without at the same time incorporating other aspects of western civilization is something only time will reveal.

For the purposes of any brief book, however, we cannot define western civilization as the entire world's civilization. Here we must work from the assumption, with a full awareness of its shortcomings, that western civilization in its more recent form, taking into account science, technology, and political power, is the civilization that has for the time reached its culmination in Europe and North America. Other nations and regions may some day displace those areas in power and cultural importance, but where and when we cannot now know. For that reason we must look backward into history at the various strands of historical development that have led to the emergence of western civilization in the North Atlantic world and try to indicate which of them appear to have been of major significance. We therefore examine the history of western civilizations with reference to:

1. Human control over the world of nature (the material environment).
2. Belief in an ordered, purposeful universe and historical progress.

3. The expansion of Europe.
4. The problem of power; the emergence of the mass-oriented state as the political form of western civilization.

Let us turn now to defining these strands of development, these themes.

1. Human Control over the World of Nature (the Material Environment)

This first theme runs implicitly through the whole history of any civilization, and hence of western civilization. When man made the first crude tools and weapons and later found out how to raise plant foods and to domesticate animals, he was no longer dependent for gaining his food or for protecting himself upon the chance opportunities offered by nature. He had taken the first slow steps in the direction of winning some control over the environment in which he lived. Since the Neolithic Revolution (which is still regarded by many historians as the most significant phase in the history of human development), when humans first discovered how to domesticate animals and crops, man—and particularly western man—has increased his skills and knowledge, not always in a steady, progressive way but often by fits and starts, until with the coming of the modern Industrial Revolutions he has achieved a control over nature which, in our own time, seems to promise a possible extension of some human control beyond the planet where man originated.

Along with his technological development man has created certain institutions and social customs which have also helped to increase his control over the material world. Though his sense of co-operation has not enabled him to avoid wars, man has, nonetheless, found ways of working with his fellows that give him an increasing measure of protection against natural disasters, against other forms of life, and even against other human beings. As a consequence, his species has now become one of the most numerous on earth.

2. Belief in an Ordered, Purposeful Universe and Historical Progress

For many historians one of the important reasons why western man has been fairly successful in his attempts to control nature is that he has developed certain ways of thinking about the world in which he lives. At various stages of his history he has assumed that the universe is an orderly place where all is done according to a divine or natural law which exists over and above the welter of human affairs and behind which there is a purpose which generally works for the best despite all the contradictions and evils that seem to exist in the daily world. While this assumption of an ordered universe may not be entirely unique to western thought, it is, nevertheless, one outstanding characteristic and seems to derive from two main sources: first, from the Judaic tradition, later carried over into Christianity, that all of history is subject to the divine law of God; and, second, from the Greek intellectual tradition which thought of the world, in spite of the diversity and disorder of everyday life, as a place governed by harmonious, mathemetical laws. These two ideas, though they have often seemed contradictory, were, on the contrary, actually complementary; for they combined to form an intellectual tradition which is usually defined as "rational." What this latter term means is that not only is the universe governed by laws but that man is possessed of a "reasoning faculty" or "reason" which makes it possible for him to understand these laws and their workings. In this sense, the world is not an unknown or unknowable place controlled by sheer chance or by capricious spirits but one in which man, by placing himself voluntarily in harmony with divine or natural laws, can hope to exercise some control over his own destiny.

In the presence of this belief in an ordered and purposeful universe western man has customarily thought about "history"—that is to say, his own past and future—in a distinctive way. Since the days of the Hebrews and the Greeks he has developed what is sometimes called "historical consciousness," a sense of past and future, of knowing that things are not always alike and the same. The idea of change in human history is an inportant one, for many societies have never developed such a conception but think of history only as a passage of time in which all things—beliefs, customs, ideas—remain essentially the same from one age to another. For western man, however, the idea of historical change has usually implied movement toward some great divine event or a better world in the future: in Christian terms, the last judgment and the everlasting life; in secular thought, the worldly utopia where all men would live out their lives in moral perfection and material abundance. This faith in historical purpose and change, whether cast in religious or secular terms, has had important social consequences, for it has helped to spur western man onward to what he has generally, though not always, believed will be a better future. At the same time it has reconciled him to the fact of and the necessity for continuous change in his existence. While he has not always accepted such change quickly or happily, he, nonetheless, has accustomed himself to it and has come to believe in it to such an extent that it has often stimulated him to alter his material circumstances and to feel that in most instances change is good. Out of this feeling has grown that faith in human progress which has dominated and still strongly influences much of modern western thought.

3. The Expansion of Europe

A third significant theme of western history has to do with the growth or expansion of Europe. Usually, this term is applied to the movement which began about the year 1500 when the first great voyages of discovery opened up distant non-European areas to European conquest, settlement, and trade. Actually, however, the age of discovery, for all its importance, was only one phase in a much more general kind of expansion that has had both internal and external aspects. For the expansion of Europe has involved not simply the movement of European people and wealth to remote parts of the earth but also an internal expansion which began well before the great age of discovery in the 16th and 17th centuries and has continued to our own day. This expansion, whose beginnings have been traced back as far as the opening of the 11th century, is characterized by five major developments: (1) growth of population; (2) rise of towns and cities (increasing urbanization); (3) colonization, first, of unsettled areas within Europe and, later, of extensive areas overseas; (4) a revolution in agricultural techniques which gradually increased the production of food; and (5) the growth of capital wealth (that is, an accumulation of goods or money used to expand economic or business activity and thus further increase production). The last of these developments is of great significance, because the European concept of capital investment (capitalism), while it has had some good and bad effects, is one of the important economic inventions of all time and has led to a process by which economic production has continuously increased and new wealth has been steadily added to society. In varying degrees all of the five above aspects of Europe's expansion have contributed to a general process of growth throughout western civilization not only in population but also in standards of living, in knowledge, and in political power.

What was ultimately most significant about Europe's internal expansion, however, was that it prepared the way for the discovery and colonization of vast regions beyond the seas. Without the long gestation of internal expansion from the early middle ages onward there would have been no possibility of Europe's breaking through the cultural isolation that characterized most human societies down to the year 1500. Wealth, technology, and the political organization of the national monarchy all played an important part, and all were developments of medieval origin.

While these indirectly made outward expansion possible, Europeans still had to be motivated toward the great effort of discovery and colonization. Undoubtedly, Christian missionary zeal had strong influences, particularly among the Portuguese and Spaniards. So, too, did the more mundane desire for riches. But neither of these was a peculiarly European motivation. Nor did Europeans at the moment when expansion began have either skills or wealth beyond those possessed by some other societies. The great Chinese empire, for example, as well as several Islamic societies might also have made the effort. Islam, after all, was scarcely less zealous than Christianity in its desire to convert the heathen. Chinese, Indian, or Arab traders were as anxious for wealth. Why, then, did Europe make the first moves toward creating a world community and civilization? The answer seems to lie in the fact that European motives were not only intense but that European consciousness of the unknown for some mysterious reason stimulated the curiosity and moved Europeans to action as other societies were not so stimulated or moved.

The result of this complex combination of causes was extremely significant for world history. Indeed, it was European expansion that first made all the isolated cultures of the earth conscious not only of themselves but of the world as a whole. Ultimately, the great success of European civilization with its utilization of science and technology, in particular, was to give to all the earth for the first time a true worldwide civilization.

4.   The Problem of Power: the Emergence of the Mass-Oriented State as the Political Form of Western Civilization

Our last major theme, one which many historians regard as among the most important, is that which deals with western man's efforts to control himself and his fellows in their workaday relations with one another. The problems of political power and the relations of the individual with the state are not, of course, things with which western man alone has had to cope. These problems are as old as organized society. What is peculiar to western man in this respect, however, is his attempt to solve the problem of political power by recognizing, formally or actually, the right of the adult mass of human beings to control or influence the state and its decisions. Also recognized, so implicitly that it remains unstated in most discussions, is the function of the state to serve the desires or at least the welfare of its people. And while it is true that not all the states of the western world are what we somewhat inaccurately call "democracies," any western government now in existence would pretend that in the ultimate its great concern is with the total well-being of all its people. Even the most totalitarian regimes justify their existence on those grounds.

One of our concerns, then, is to understand how it was that this assumption of mass control or mass welfare came to dominate the political thinking and to a large extent the political practice of the West. In part, it may be explained by the evolution of monarchial government in early modern history (16th through the 18th century), when kings ceased to be the limited, personal rulers of feudal monarchies and became instead the theoretically all-powerful heads of a state apparatus which regulated and controlled the lives of their subjects. In the course of this change, however, European monarchs found themselves facing strong opposition from an ever-growing body of subjects. At first, the royal claims to power were resisted by the old feudal nobility, who resented the assumption of complete political authority by the crown. Later, as wealth increased and the level of literacy rose, other classes and groups in various countries of Europe also joined in the resistance to royal authority. These persons, who generally belonged to the professional and business classes more frequently described as the "middle class" (though the term is somewhat vague), actually prepared the way for the great democratic mass movements of the 19th and 20th centuries. This they could not have done, however, had not a further increase in wealth and production, attendant upon the industrialization of Europe from the 18th century onward, made it possible to raise the literacy level of the masses and to increase the political consciousness of large numbers of ordinary human beings. The end result is that western civilization has been able to develop a social and political awareness that has worked in favor of the "common man" to an extent unknown in any previous historic period.

CHAPTER 2

Man and His Past

THE ESSENTIAL MOVEMENT

Human civilization fills a relatively short span in the biological history of mankind and an infinitesimally short one in the geological history of the planet. Man is a late comer to the world scene. His achievements during the few hundred millenia of his existence are remarkable when one considers the fairly long periods during which other organisms dominated the earth. Man has, quite literally, exploded into biological prominence. He has detailed knowledge of only one small part of his history, roughly five thousand recent years; he can only infer or deduce from anthropological or archeological evidence just what the various stages were through which his prehistoric ancestors passed before they became conscious that they had a future and a past. Astonishingly, despite the seemingly vast accretion of modern knowledge, men really know little about themselves, their origins, or their early evolution. The human race lives in a flash of consciousness isolated from the darkness of the past and the uncertainty of the future. For men, the greatest riddle is still that of human existence. How was it that man came to be in all the vastness of a seemingly impersonal universe? What is the purpose, if any, in his being where he is? In these questions lie the elements of the greatest of all detective stories. Men have sought for bits and pieces of clues from the beginning of recorded time, and though the evidence has mounted, we are still far from any final answer. Each generation turns anew to the excitement and mystery of it; and each, in looking backward across

EVENTS AND DEFINITIONS

A.   The Origins of Man in the Paleolithic Period

Prehistoric Cultural Periods

Dates given in this chapter are only broad approximations, since scholars have not perfected nor agreed upon the dating of prehistoric periods. Furthermore, cultural periods overlap—in some parts even of today's world the Urban Revolution has scarcely appeared; indeed, some peoples are still in the period of Stone Age culture.

The Paleolithic (Old Stone) Period, perhaps a million years in duration, ending about 12,000 B.C.

Comprised probably 99% of man's life on earth; all the periods since make up 1%. Men used fire and lived by hunting and collecting fruits and vegetables. No agriculture, no domestic animals. Tools of bone or stone and probably of wood, but no metals and no pottery.

1.   Lower Paleolithic, to about 50,000 B.C.

Four known types of men appear to have lived in this period: Pithecanthropus (Java Man) and Sinanthropus (Peking Man), both about 500,000 years ago, as well as the Neanderthal and his cousins, both about 150,000 years ago. They had crude stone tools formed by chipping or flaking (eoliths or "dawn stones").

2.   Upper Paleolithic, c. 50,000 to c. 12,000 B.C.

First true man (*Homo sapiens*) appeared: Grimaldi man in southern Europe and Cro-Magnon man further north, Cro-Magnon man created sophisticated bone tools and cave paintings, c. 20,000 B.C.

human history, seeks to add some previously unknown piece of evidence or some new hypothesis that may bring men sure knowledge about their own beginnings. Whether this goal will ever be reached we cannot now know. For those who think the answers to the Big Questions about man are worth knowing, the excitement of the search is enough to justify it.

A. The Origins of Man in the Paleolithic Period

From everything that we know of human beings under every historical condition, it is clear that men have always lived under some kind of social organization for two elemental and obvious purposes. First, because they had to subsist: to find food, shelter, and the basic necessities that make life possible. Second, because men have needed protection against the forces of nature and against their fellow men. Both of these elemental needs, subsistence and protection, have given rise over many thousands of years to the various forms of human economic and political organization. It should not be assumed, however, that man, through all of this long social evolution, was simply the creature of blind chance or forces beyond his control. His traditions and institutions were also the result of a conscious creative effort over which his moral aspirations and his standards of value exerted a powerful influence.

**B. The Advance of Man since the Paleolithic Period:
    The Neolithic Revolution**

1. Mesolithic (Middle Stone) Period, c. 12,000 to c. 8000 B.C.

Recession of the last glacier; dog domesticated; bow and arrow used.

2. Neolithic (New Stone) Period, c. 8000 to 5000 B.C.

There has long been a great deal of discussion among scholars as to where the Neolithic Revolution first occurred on earth. The reason for doubt is that primitive man wherever he first organized into communities had some of the skills that characterize the Neolithic Revolution. For the present, however, the consensus of opinion is that the great transformation of the Neolithic period probably occurred first in southwestern Asia in regions near to or encompassed by the two great rivers, Tigris and Euphrates, and the region of the Indus. Why it should have first occurred in those regions is still a matter for conjecture. Two suggestions have been made. First, that this was a region in which wild cereals, later domesticated into agricultural crops, flourished in a natural state. In brief, it is believed that men, in observing the cycle of growth of these wild cereals by trial and error hit upon the idea of gathering and planting cereal seeds. Second, it is also conjectured that the inhabitants of this region were driven to undertake domestic agriculture by necessity. Evidence seems to indicate that the region passed through a prolonged period of drouth as a result of major climatic changes. This drouth forced men to think of new expedients for survival. One of these expedients may have been domestic agriculture. Whatever the case, the archeological record seems to indicate that this region developed the oldest existing village communities of a kind that would not have been possible without agricultural skills.

The four major cultural attainments of the Neolithic Revolution, which is still perhaps the most important in human history were: (1) agriculture (2) domesticated animals; (3) pottery; and (4) polished (rather than chipped) stone tools.

The great fact of the Neolithic Revolution was that it enabled man to produce a surplus of food for his ordinary needs for the first time in history.

B. The Advance of Man since the Paleolithic Period: The Neolithic Revolution

In the earliest periods of human history, because men lacked highly developed skills and techniques, it was necessary to devote almost all of human activity to the winning of subsistence or to the protection of self, family, or tribe. With time, men acquired more highly developed skills and expanded their political organization so that relatively less time and effort had to be devoted to subsistence or protection. As a consequence, human beings were able to turn their attention to other things—literature, art, learning—which were not immediately useful in the winning of bread or in warding off enemies. Furthermore, as human social organization became more complex, the time required for the acquisition of social skills and techniques had to be extended, and education came to be an important part of social life. In time, too, it was less necessary for every able-bodied person to participate directly in the gathering or growing of food, so that men were able to diversify their social organization in such a way that some persons became specialists in technique. This development had two important results: first, it led to the formation of a specialized social system with a class structure whose various components usually had a specific function to fulfill; and, second, it ultimately made possible the greater concentration of human population in towns and cities.

Almost all of these changes occurred before the beginning of recorded history as a result of two great revolutions in human activity.

The first of these is usually called the Neolithic Revolution because it was the culmination of a development at the end of the Stone Age by which men became food producers rather than food gatherers. Men learned to improve their earliest stone tools by grinding and polishing; they also learned to domesticate animals and to cultivate crops, achievements which made them far less dependent upon the caprices of nature and thus gave them, in a limited way, some control over their environment. As a result of the Neolithic Revolution the number of humans who could survive to raise families was enormously increased, and men spread themselves over the face of the earth into virtually every area that was capable of supporting human life.

C. The Advance of Man into the Urban Revolution

1. Chalcolithic (Copper and Stone) Period, c. 5000 to c. 3500 B.C.

   Era of transition when metalworking began to be fairly common.

2. Bronze Age begins, c. 3500 B.C.

   Use of copper-tin alloys marked the beginning of metallurgy and probably also the beginning of a more complex social organization leading up to the Urban Revolution.

3. Urban Revolution, c. 3000 B.C.

   The achievements of the Neolithic Revolution made possible the emergence of a more sophisticated and complex social organization. Villages came into being, and, in time, villages gradually expanded into the larger units we know as cities. The city was a diversified, interdependent social unit whose existence depended upon the development of various kinds of specialized skills. Moreover, the city was a social organism which could not support itself without access to surplus foods and raw materials not produced within the city itself. Cities therefore had to live by specialized manufacture and external trade. The growth of specialization brought into being various groups previously unknown to rural communities or even villages. Artisans, priests, officials, soldiers could not have existed in previous communities. Furthermore, the complexities of city life, the needs of government, commerce, and manufacture, required literacy. Without literacy in the forms of writing, reading, and mathematics it would have been impossible to conduct trade across great distances or to govern larger territories. It is not surprising, therefore, that the emergence of city life throughout the Near and Middle East sometime around 4000 B.C. also ushered in the beginnings of written language and the development of arithmetical skills.

4. Iron Age begins, c. 1800 B.C.

   Last major stage in the early development of metallurgy.

C.   The Advance of Man into the Urban Revolution

Following the Neolithic Revolution mankind appears to have passed through two stages of technological development leading up to and coincident with the rise of city life. The first of these stages is usually described as the Bronze Age because it was during this period that men first began to make use of metals, specifically of copper and tin, which go into the making of bronze. The second stage saw the introduction of ironworking and is, therefore, known as the Iron Age. Using these metals—stronger and more durable than stone—men began to develop tools and skills which, in their turn, made possible the Urban Revolution: the emergence of that more complex social form known as a civilization.

At this point we need to understand what the words culture and civilization mean. Despite a great many differences among scholars, the term culture is most frequently employed to describe the social life of a community in a preliterate stage, that is, before it has acquired the skills of reading and writing. Civilization, on the other hand, is commonly descriptive of communities that have reached the stage of literacy and have developed a number of the complex ideas (art and science, for example) and institutions which give society a measure of stability and efficiency in the handling of social problems.

The city is pre-eminently the symbol of civilization. With the coming of city life, the community ceases to be a small, isolated, homogeneous, self-sufficient unit. The division of labor is no longer simple. Relationships among human beings transcend personal or family ties and become impersonal and indirect. The city itself is dependent upon, but exists in partial isolation from, the surrounding countryside. Its ideas and values are often very different, and, in the long run, a city's influence will often transform its rural surroundings completely. Once the city has come into being, man is equipped with a social organization capable of transmitting new ideas and innovations across great distances, for the city becomes not only the great innovator of civilizations but also the means by which they are spread across the world.

EVENTS AND DEFINITIONS

A. The Civilization of the Tigris-Euphrates Region (Mesopotamia)

1. Early Copper Age, c. 4500-3000 B.C.

   Invention of writing; period of primitive democratic societies.

2. Early Sumerian Civilization; hegemony of Akkadians, c. 3000-2000 B.C.

   Formation of separate city-states by about 3000 B.C. Akkadians under Sargon and Naram-Sin ruled over most of Sumeria, c. 2400-2250 B.C. Sumerians disappeared as a separate people, c. 2000 B.C.

CHAPTER 3

The Early Civilizations
of the Eastern Mediterranean

THE ESSENTIAL MOVEMENT

The oldest civilizations known to western man are those two which grew up in the great river-valley systems of the Nile and the Tigris-Euphrates. Both areas provided an environment (soil, water, climatic conditions) conducive to a high level of social development. There, so far as we know, man gained his earliest experience of civilized urban life.

A. The Civilizations of the Tigris-Euphrates Region (Mesopotamia)

Between the Tigris and Euphrates rivers in what is now the kingdom of Iraq appeared the first sophisticated urban societies created by the Neolithic Revolution. There, a sweeping arc of land watered by the two great rivers and known as the fertile crescent cradled the societies out of which later western civilization was to evolve. Unlike Egypt, which is discussed in the next section, the Tigris-Euphrates was not defined by the clear geophysical limits of a single river valley. The rivers flowed for long distances through open plains and were neither so easily managed for human use nor so predictable in their flood stages as the Nile. This somewhat harsher environment helped to form a system of beliefs and institutions very different from those of ancient Egypt. In general, the gods of Mesopotamia (another

Sumerian religion: The earliest Mesopotamian historical records reveal that the first social units were temple communities which the king and the priests ruled as agents of the gods. Thus there was no such thing in ancient Mesopotamia as a secular state in the modern sense. The life of the people was controlled and permeated by religion as fully as was the life of Egypt but with an important difference. While the gods of Egypt tended, on the whole, to be beneficent, the gods of Sumer were not only capricious but, in a sense, indifferent to man's fate. According to the Sumerian legend of creation, mankind was created to serve the gods. Man was thus a slave to divine authority, and even kings were only stewards responsive to the will of the gods. The gods were worshipped out of fear and submission and not because men loved them. Nor were the gods of Mesopotamia looked upon as just and powerful protectors who rewarded good and punished evil. The gods, in fact, did not protect the land nor behave justly to its inhabitants. They demanded much of their worshippers and gave little in return. The important thing, however, was that believers should continually offer sacrifices to the gods only to avoid divine wrath. The gods, furthermore, never made it clear just what they wanted from their followers. It was up to ordinary men to guess what the gods wanted of them and woe betide if they were wrong. In this respect the gods of Mesopotamia differed from the Hebrews' conception of divinity. The Hebrew God required certain things of his people but always made it perfectly clear just what it was he expected. As a result, the ancient Hebrews even in times of tribulation always had a sense of confidence and security that the Sumerians never possessed. The Sumerian sense of pessimism was perhaps best expressed in the *Epic of Gilgamesh* where the hero overcomes great difficulties in a search for immortality only to lose the precious gift in the end by sheer chance. The lesson of the great epic is plain. There is no end for man in this world but death.

3.   Babylonian Supremacy, c. 2000-910 B.C.

A. RULE OF THE AMORITES, C. 2000-1750 B.C. Babylon asserted supremacy over most of the Tigris-Euphrates Region; Marduk became chief god of Mesopotamia; Code of Hammurabi formulated, *c.* 1800 B.C.

name for the region) were less benign and more capricious than the Egyptian deities. As a consequence, the literature of the early Mesopotamian peoples is filled wtth with a pessimistic fear of the inexplicable wrath of the gods.

In the earliest known stages of its history the civilization of Mesopotamia was dominated by the Sumerians, who lived in a confederation of city-states which were finally brought together under the rule of a single people, the Akkadians, about 3000 B.C. The hegemony of the Akkadians was followed by a series of other foreign conquests until sometime around 2300 B.C., when the city of Ur was able to achieve independence and bring the other Sumerian cities under its control. Around 2000 B.C. a new group of conquerors, the Amorites, captured Babylon on the Euphrates and gradually made this small village into the center of the Sumerian world. During the period immediately following the Amorite conquest the city-god of Babylon, Marduk, supplanted the other deities of Sumer, and Hammurabi, the sixth king of the new dynasty, gave a famous code of laws to the whole Tigris-Euphrates region. After Hammurabi's death about 1750 B.C. a new band of barbarians, the Kassites, conquered Babylon and ruled it and the surrounding territories until the kingdom of Assyria emerged as the dominant power of the Middle East in the 10th century B.C.

With the coming of the Assyrians the whole of the eastern Mediterranean area was for the first time united into a single great empire. The latter, by their ruthless passion for conquest and the harshness with which they treated defeated peoples, were to be remembered as the most hated conquerors of the ancient world. Nonetheless, their military and administrative skills have to be admired, for these enabled the Assyrians to branch out from their capital at Nineveh on the upper reaches of the Tigris to bring Mesopotamia, Palestine, and Egypt under their control during the 8th and 7th centuries B.C. In the end, their capacity as conquerors exceeded their ability to control the territories they had absorbed. Their final defeat came toward the end of the 7th century at the hands of the Chaldeans, who had settled in the southeastern corner of the Tigris-Euphrates valley.

The empire built by the Chaldeans, in spite of its great cultural achievements, was short-lived. Internal decay led to its easy overthrow in 538 B.C. by Cyrus (600?-529 B.C.), the Great King of the Medes and Persians, and the foundation by these latter peoples of another great empire stretching from the Hellespont to the river Indus. This conquest led to the merging of the civilizations of the ancient Mesopotamian and Mediterranean worlds into the main stream of western civilization, for

B. RULE OF THE KASSITES, C. 1750-910 B.C.

4. Assyrian Empire, c. 910-606 B.C.

Conquest of Babylon by Assyrians (910 B.C.). Conquest of Samaria and deportation of its inhabitants, *c*. 721 B.C. Conquest of Egypt by Esar-Haddon, *c*. 670 B.C. Assyrians defeated and their empire overthrown at Battle of Carchemish, c. 606 B.C.

5. Chaldeans and New Babylonians, 606-538 B.C.

Nebuchadnezzar conquered Jerusalem, 586 B.C. Persian conquest of Oabyln, 538 B.C.

6. Persian Empire, c. 600-330 B.C.

Prophet Zoroaster preached a highly ethical and humane religion, c. 600 B.C. Conquest of Egypt by Persians, 525 B.C. Attempts to conquer Greece by Darius the Great (521-486 B.C.) and Xerxes (486-465 B.C.) defeated at Marathon (490 B.C.) and Salamis (480 B.C.). Alexander the Great conquered Persia, 330 B.C.

7. The Mesopotomian Cultural Achievement.

The importance of the Mesopotamian cultural achievement as this evolved from ancient Sumer to the Persians is difficult to exaggerate. The peoples of the region developed the first writing, the first true alphabet, commercial organization, city-state government, weights and measures, a numbering system based upon the unit 60 which later resulted in the 360-degree circle, and a codified system of law.

B. The Egyptian Civilization

1. Old Kingdom: Dynasties I-VI, c. 3000-2200 B.C.

Union of Upper and Lower Egypt, *c*. 3200 B.C. First great era of pyramid building (Great Pyramid of Cheops or Khufu, *c*. 2600 B.C.). Evolution of the divine kingship of Pharaoh.

it was Darius the Great (521-486 B.C.) who, having usurped the Persian throne on the death of Cyrus's successor, conquered Egypt and attempted the conquest of a part of Europe in a series of unsuccessful campaigns against the Greek city-states.

While it is impossible to say just how much the various societies of the Tigris-Euphrates region and the later empires into which they were absorbed influenced Hellenic (Greek) civilization and thus, ultimately, the civilization of the western world, there seems little doubt but that there must have been a great deal of interchange which had lasting effects. The Mesopotamian civilization was a seed-bed of numerous important religions, including Zorastrianism and Mithraism, both of which had certain elements in common with Judaism and Christianity and both of which later penetrated deeply into the Roman world. In other areas of culture, particularly astronomy and mathematics (in which latter the Mesopotamian civilizations appear to have excelled even the Egyptians), the influence was at least as great. Finally, it should be remembered that both the Assyrian and Persian empires developed the art of government to a level not again to be achieved in the Mediterranean world until the emergence of imperial Rome.

B.   The Egyptian Civilization

Far to the west of the Tigris-Euphrates region in the long narrow valley of the Nile which extended for hundreds of miles inland from the Mediterranean shoreline at the extreme northeastern corner of Africa appeared another of the first true civilizations. Protected by the surrounding desert and served by the river, the ancient inhabitants of Egypt, at a very early period, developed a high level of agriculture which in turn made it possible for the valley to support a fairly dense population and to build up a complex but highly stable society that lasted for nearly twenty-five hundred years.

2.　First Intermediate Period: Dynasties VII-XI, c. 2200-2000 B.C.

Breakdown of central government caused disunity and localized rule.

3.　Middle Kingdom: Dynasty XII, c. 2000-1790 B.C.

High point of Egyptian civilization; strong central government; relatively high standard of living.

4.　Second　Intermediate　Period:　Dynasties　XIII-XVII, c. 1790-1550 B.C.

Egypt conquered by the Hyksos (Shepherd Kings); reconquered by Theban princes.

5.　New Kingdom: Period of Imperial Expansion, Dynasties XVIII-XX, c. 1550-1090 B.C.

Conquest of Syria and part of Mesopotamia by Thutmose III (*c.* 1490-1436 B.C.) at the battle of Megiddo (*c.* 1468 B.C.).

A. BOOK OF THE DEAD, C. 1400 B.C. Appearance of the *Book of the Dead* in its final form; contained spells and magic formulas for entering into life after death.

B. THE RELIGIOUS REVOLUTION OF AKHNATON (IKHNATON), 14TH CENTURY B.C. Amenhotep IV (c. 1377-1360 B.C.) took the name Akhnaton and tried to substitute the new, more ethically developed religion of Aton for that of Amon. Bitter resistance by the priesthood of Amon led to the restoration of the older religion after Akhnaton's death.

The cult of Aton has often been looked upon as truly monotheistic and ethical in the same sense as the religion of the ancient Hebrews. In the two great hymns to Aton which have survived there are, indeed, some evidences of monotheism. Aton is frequently represented as the only real god who gives and conserves life. He is also a universal and beneficent god who has been fully revealed in the heart of Akhnaton himself. Nevertheless, Aton was not like the divinities of the great monotheistic religions. He remained a nature god, as is revealed by the hymns themselves. While the latter emphasize the importance of truth, they have no great ethical content. In this respect, they differ very markedly from the

The political history of ancient Egypt begins with the union of the Upper and Lower Kingdoms under a single ruler about 3200 B.C. From that time onward Egyptian history is marked into periods according to the dynasties that ruled the country. The first six of these constituted the period of the Old Kingdom (c. 3000-2200 B.C.), when a high level of civilization was first attained. Over some centuries, during the period of the Old Kingdom, the Egyptian concept of divine government evolved, and the king or pharaoh came to be looked upon as the personification of divinity. Accordingly, every form of political and social activity was pervaded with religious feeling.

After the downfall of the Old Kingdom and a period of anarchy from the VIIth through the XIth dynasties (c. 2200-2000 B.C.), the shattered power of the pharaohs was restored; and a new period, that of the Middle Kingdom (c. 2000-1790 B.C.), began. The Middle Kingdom marks the high point of Egyptian civilization when the mass of the people seem to have enjoyed good government and a relatively high level of prosperity. Its end came with conquest by the nomadic Hyksos who ruled the country during the Second Intermediate Period (c. 1790-1550 B.C.). When, in time, the Egyptians learned to use the military techniques of their conquerors, native rule was gradually restored and the last great period of Egyptian history began, that of the New Kingdom (c. 1550-1090 B.C.).

Under the dynasts of the New Kingdom much of the former strength of the pharaohs was recovered and Egypt, through the conquests of her rulers, became a great imperial power. With this external transformation, Egyptian society underwent several changes. For the first time the cultural isolation of the country was broken as Egyptians came into contact with alien societies. Increased military obligations and a great influx of foreign slaves created a new society where there was greater cleavage between rich and poor. And, finally, the priesthood of Amon (supreme god among the deities of Egypt) grew so rich and powerful that it tempted the Pharaoh Amenhotep IV, also known as Akhnaton or Ikhnaton, to break its power (c. 1375). To do so, he tried to bring about a religious revolution by emphasizing monotheism (worship of one god) instead of the traditional polytheism (worship of many gods) of his people. Ultimately he was defeated, but the victory of the priesthood was costly. In the end, it led to the degeneration of religious belief and a consequent decline in the whole of Egyptian civilization.

By about 1150 B.C., the great Egyptian empire had begun to break up. During the next four centuries Egypt was, once again, ruled by a succession of foreign conquerors. Independence was restored for a brief great Hebrew Psalms and prophecies. Indeed, though the history of Egyptian religion indicates that there was a great deal of ethical growth over a long period of time, ethical standards remained distinctly selfish. They stressed material rewards here or in the hereafter and magnified the importance of human approval for one's personal conduct. There was little notion that duty and righteousness were good things in and of themselves. Magic was supremely important in the affairs of men both in this world and the next. The whole elaborate Osirian ritual of the dead seems, in fact, to have been designed as a means of deceiving the divine judge. For all of this, however, it must be admitted that the Egyptians had some sense of the moral order of things centuries before other peoples of the ancient world did.

c. EGYPTIAN CULTURAL ACHIEVEMENT. The Egyptians were not great theoreticians in the field of science. They were, rather, very shrewd observers who derived a great deal of their learning from practical experience. Their system of mathematics, though cumbersome, was, nonetheless, accurate, and they were able to use it very skillfully in engineering calculations. The greatest of their construction achievements, the Great Pyramid of Cheops (Khufu), in its measurements indicates that they possessed mathematical knowledge which would not be known in the western world until centuries later. Their literature was not generally good narrative, because its purpose was not to tell a story but to teach timeless truths. Perhaps their greatest achievements were in the realm of architecture where they were the first ancient people to employ stone in massive construction.

6. New Kingdom Post-imperial period: Dynasties XXI-XXX, c. 1090-525 B.C.

Conquest of Egypt by the Assyrians (c. 670 B.C.); by Persia (525 B.C.); and by Alexander the Great (332 B.C.).

C. The Eastern Maritime Civilizations and the Ancient Hebrews

1. Aegean (Cretan or Minoan) Civilization. c. 3000-1200 B.C.

Minoan civilization flourished on Crete, *c.* 3000-1200 B.C. Mycenean (named for its capital at Mycenae) civilization period during the 7th and 6th centuries B.C., only to be lost to the conquering Persians in 525 B.C.

Like most ancient civilizations, that of Egypt was deeply rooted in religious belief. Under what seems to have been environmental influence, the Egyptians developed a body of rites which symbolized, on the one hand, the rise and fall of the river (cult of Osiris) and, on the other, the power of the life-giving sun (cult of Ra). The worship of Ra became the basis for the divine authority of the pharaohs, while that of Osiris gave rise to the cult of the dead with its elaborate tomb building and mummification. Over the centuries a fairly steady progression from polytheism to monotheism is noticeable in Egyptian religious history; and with it a greater stress on ethical teaching also developed.

It is difficult to say whether Egyptian civilization had an important direct influence on the western world. Its literature was extensive, and its achievements in mathematics (particularly in surveying and measurement), engineering (the great tombs and pyramids), and medicine are impressive even by modern standards. How much of this was transmitted directly to western civilization we can only guess, since most of the learning of ancient Egypt had first to pass through the hands of the Greeks and Romans, who did not always acknowledge the Egyptian sources. Nonetheless, Egypt's great accomplishments over more than two thousand years cannot have failed to make an impact on her neighbors.

C.   The Eastern Maritime Civilizations and the Ancient Hebrews

Along the shores and in the islands of the eastern Mediterranean there grew up, from about 2000 B.C. onward, a spectrum of cultures, partly maritime and partly pastoral. The two most famous of the former were those of the Minoans, builders of a great oceanic empire (thalasappeared on Greek mainland before 1600 B.C. Conquest of Crete by Dorian invaders, *c.* 1200 B.C. Dark age of Aegean civilization in Crete and on Greek mainland, *cg* 1100-800 B.C.

2. Hittites, 3000-1200 B.C.

Settled in northern Asia Minor; Hittite Empire reached its height about 1900 B.C.; overthrown about 1200 B.C.

3. Phoenicians, sometime before 2000 to 332 B.C.

Settled in Palestine sometime before 2000 B.C. Reached the high point of maritime supremacy, *c.* 1000-774 B.C. Their city, Tyre, conquered by Alexander the Great, 332 B.C.

4. Aramaeans, c. 1500-732 B.C.

First appeared in Palestine about 1500 B.C. Established Kingdom of Damascus (*c.* 1000-732 B.C.). Damascus conquered by Assyrians, 732 B.C.

5. Lydian Empire, c. 950-547 B.C.

Emerged about 1000 B.C. in northern Asia Minor. Absorbed into Persian Empire, *c.* 547 B.C.

6. Hebrews, c. 2000 B.C.-135 A.D.

Exodus of Hebrews from Egypt, *c.* 1260 B.C. Period of Judges in Israel, *c.* 1225-1020 B.C. Saul, King of Israel, 1020-1004 B.C. David, 1004-965 B.C. Solomon, 965-926 B.C. Division of Israel, 926 B.C. Exile of the Hebrews in Babylon, 586-538 B.C. Conquest of Palestine by Alexander the Great, 332 B.C., and by Antiochus III of Syria, 198 B.C. Revolt of the Maccabees against Antiochus IV, 167 B.C.

Roman conquest of Palestine, 63 B.C. Jewish revolt against Romans, 66-70 A.D. Destruction of Jerusalem by Emperor Titus, 70 A.D. Jews not permitted to live in rebuilt city of Jerusalem; beginning of dispersion (diaspora) of the Jewish people, 135 A.D.

The Evolution of the Hebraic Religious Tradition: One of the interesting problems of ancient history is the question of why it was that the ancient Hebrews (who later established the kingdoms of Israel and Judah) came to think of their God as a single deity whose authority extended not just over the socracy) based upon the island of Crete, whose civilization lasted from about 3000 B.C. to 1200 B.C., and the Phoenicians, famous traders who occupied a narrow coastal strip of Palestine and Syria which contained the great cities of Tyre and Sidon. To the north of the Phoenicians were the lands held by the Hittites (c. 3000-1200 B.C.) and the kingdom of Lydia which was absorbed into the Persian empire about 547 B.C. Because of their close connection with the ancient Hebrews, a more important people in this general area were the Aramaeans, who were apparently one of the several Semitic tribes that first moved into Palestine about 1500 B.C. Like the Phoenicians they founded a mercantile community, whose major city was Damascus. The social resiliency and commercial importance of the Aramaeans kept them from absorption by various conquerors and over some centuries enabled them to spread their influence so widely throughout the Near East that in time their language became the common tongue of many diverse peoples and was spoken even by Jesus Christ.

Among all the peoples of the Near Eastern world, however, none was destined to a greater historical future than the Hebrew inhabitants of the Biblical land of Canaan, despite the fact that they were neither so powerful nor so cultivated as the great states which surrounded them; for the Hebrews, like the Greeks and Romans who followed after them, were to contribute significantly to western civilization. Much of what we know about the early history of this people is derived from conjecture based upon their cumulative historical-religious records known to the western world as the Old Testament. From what later generations have been able to reconstruct on the basis of Biblical scholarship and archeology, it seems plain that the Hebrews, after some centuries of warfare during which a part of their number was carried off into Egypt, founded the community of Israel sometime in the 13th century B.C. After a long process of evolution the various tribes of early Hebrews organized a strong kingdom which reached its peak during the successive reigns of Saul, David, and Solomon (c. 1020-926 B.C.). With Solomon's death, the kingdom was divided into two separate states: Israel in the north and Judah in the south. In the 8th century B.C. the northern kingdom was absorbed by Assyria. In the south, however, Judah proved more resilient; and there the Hebrew tradition was preserved, despite successive conquests by Chaldeans, Persians, and Romans. Until their final dispersion by the Romans in 70 A.D. the Hebrews or Jews (from the name Judah) augmented and expanded the religious tradition that was to make them one of the great peoples of history.

In the sphere of religion this small hill people offered the world

Israelites but over all of mankind. Traditionally, of course, the answer to this puzzle, so far as believing Jews and Christians have been concerned, is simple and straightforward. The ancient Hebrews and Israelites did not "invent" the conception of monotheism. Yahweh (Jehovah) was and is the one true God of all the universe. When He revealed His purposes and of monotheism. Yahwek (Jehovah) was and is the one true God of all the universe. When He revealed His purposes and His law to Abraham, He did so because the Hebrews were His people specially chosen to impart a knowledge of divine law and of Yahweh Himself to all men. The reason why Yahweh chose them for this great purpose was because they had agreed to keep His laws for all time coming. Secular historians, in the main, do not disagree with the idea that the ancient Hebrews and Israelites were unique in their monotheistic beliefs and their system of ethics. They have, however, sought to explain the "monotheistic revolution" in ancient Hebrew thought in historical rather than purely religious terms. Some scholars have suggested that the Hebrews must have been influenced by other peoples and religions in the ancient world, e.g., the Egyptian cult of Aton or Zoroastrianism. However this may be, the fact remains that Hebrew monotheism as it developed over a period of about 600 years (from the eighth to the second century B.C.) was a product of the ancient Israelite tradition alone. This development was made possible by generations of prophets ("Prophetic revolution") who preached (1) that Yahweh was a just God who demanded righteous conduct of men and who punished the wicked and (2) that He was also the God of all humanity.

something unique. Their religion, which appears to have been mono-theistic in form as far back as historical evidence runs, gradually evolved into a system of belief quite different from the beliefs of other ancient peoples. What gave to the Hebraic religion its significant qualities was a combination of three important elements: first a sense of purpose in history which, unlike the religions of Egypt or Mesopotamia, made it clear that man was not the victim of capricious gods moved by human passions but a being who was part of a divine plan in which the Hebrews, specifically, and later all the human race had a part to play; second, a belief that this great plan required the ethical co-operation of mankind (that is, that men were expected to make a choice in all their actions of good rather than evil); and, third, the assurance that the Hebrew God, Jehovah (Yahweh), was not only omnipotent (all-powerful) but all-perfect. The essence of Hebrew belief was summed up in a carefully formulated code of ritualistic laws derived from the ethical teachings of the prophet Moses (decalogue or Ten Commandments). In the end, it was the great central idea of Judaism as expressed in this code, namely, that man was responsible to God for his transgression of the law, which was carried over into Christianity and the western tradition.

EVENTS AND DEFINITIONS

A. The Greek (Hellenic) Civilization, c. 1300-338 B.C.

1. Early Invasions, c. 1300-1000 B.C.

Achaeans, Ionians, Aeolians, and Epirots, c. 1300-1100 B.C. Dorians, c. 1100-1000 B.C.

The Background of Classical Greek Civilization. Until about 100 years ago all that was known about the beginnings of Greek civilization came down to us from the ancient Greeks themselves. This knowledge was extremely limited. The Greeks like most early peoples were not great record keepers. And even if more records existed than we later knew about, these did not survive. Furthermore, the ancient Greeks did not always distinguish fact from myths or legends, so that it was necessary for scholars to reconstruct what they knew about the

CHAPTER 4

Greco-Roman Civilization

THE ESSENTIAL MOVEMENT

Two other great civilizations complete the fusion of elements in the ancient Mediterranean basin which went into the making of western civilization: Greece, where a high, almost miraculous, level of culture was reached in the 5th and 4th centuries B.C., and Rome, which, by bringing the whole Mediterranean area under its control, was destined to transmit the traditions of the ancient world to the Christian West.

A. The Greek (Hellenic) Civilization

The civilization of ancient Hellas (Greece) was centered in a geographical area made up of what is now modern Greece, the nearby islands and coastal regions of the Aegean Sea, and also settlements in western Asia Minor and along the southern shores of the Sea of Marmora. From this original homeland Greek traders and colonists moved outward until by the middle of the 6th century B.C. the Hellenes (Greeks) were scattered in settlements that extended from the Black Sea to Spain, North Africa, Europe, and Asia Minor.

The Greeks as a separately identified people first emerged on the scene of history sometime about the year 1000 B.C. Where they came from remains something of a mystery, but it is believed that successive waves of them invaded the lower Balkan peninsula and there settled in separate tribal regions named for each group of invaders (Achaeans, origins of Greek society from a few scattered sources like the writings of Homer and Hesiod. Nevertheless, for all of their limitations, these writings had an important historic effect. Homer's great poems, the *Iliad* and the *Odyssey*, helped to bring modern archeology into being. The 19th century German scholar, Heinrich Schliemann (1822-1890), was convinced that Homer's story of the siege of Troy was based upon fact. He set out to prove his hypothesis in 1870 by excavating the mount of Hissarlik in Asia Minor which he identified as the original site of Homeric Troy. Successive excavations tended to prove Schliemann right, but, more importantly, they stimulated other scholars to make use of the spade as a means of expanding our knowledge of Greek prehistory. As a result, since about 1900 we have come to know more about the ancestors of the Greeks than the ancient Greeks did themselves. What do we know? Our knowledge, even now is somewhat vague, because we must infer a great deal from archeological remains (artifacts), but still it is substantial. Moreover, a few recently discovered documents like the famous Linear B fragment have enlisted the skills of the linguistics experts who have been able to tell us something more. It is now believed that the first peoples whose descendants were the classical Greeks probably appeared in Asia Minor and the Greek mainland sometime around 2000 B.C. This, if true, suggests that the prehistory of the Greeks reaches further back into the past than previous scholars thought. Moreover, it also suggests that the great civilizations which came into being on the island of Crete and on the Greek mainland at Mycenne were in time absorbed, perhaps by conquest, into Greek society. Indeed, in the latter part of their history they probably were Greek. Sometime about 1300-1200 B.C., however, a great wave of migrations spread over the whole eastern mediterranean region. As a consequence, there occurred a number of wars of conquest in which older, long-established societies were overthrown. The brilliant Mycenean civilization was conquered by the Dorians, a people apparently of Greek stock but apparently little touched by the influences of other Greek societies. With the downfall of Mycenae and the collapse of its sophisticated system of government bureaucracy the original Greek language of the Linear B fragment appears to have been lost. Thus Greek society became illiterate and entered a "dark

Aeolians, Dorians, Epirots, and Ionians). The last of these conquerors were the Dorians, whose coming ushered in a period of transition between the end of the brilliant Mycenean civilization (an offshoot of the Minoan civilization which had expanded from Crete to the Greek mainland) and the great age of Hellenic civilization which began about the 8th century B.C. The two great epic poems of Homer, the *Iliad* and the *Odyssey*, were written toward the end of this transitional period—probably sometime between 850 and 700 B.C. These two great works were to influence the whole cast of Greek thought and action. Man, in the Homeric tradition, is a creature whose powers are limited by the laws of fate which neither he nor the gods can transcend. The most that human beings can hope to do is to live so that they will be immortalized, not in an afterlife but in the memory of posterity. Theirs is the duty to live nobly and not attempt to challenge the fates by exalting themselves. To exalt oneself is to invite the retribution of the gods who administer but do not control the laws of the universe. Within this view is contained all that is essential for Greek religious belief and all the famous elements of later Greek tragedy.

At the end of the Homeric Age the distinctive characteristics of Greek society—its great variety and its lack of political unity—were already clearly in evidence. The earliest form of political organization was probably tribal. Over a period of some centuries the tribe or clan passed over into the peculiarly Greek political unit, the city-state or polis. Each polis was self-sufficient and included both an urban core and large areas of surrounding countryside. Every freeborn Greek was born into a polis just as he was born into a family. The polis was the center of life and the focus of all community activity. In this way, the city-state came to be a social as well as a political unit, and exile from the polis became the worst of all punishments. Cut off from his native city, the Hellene became a rootless person who could rarely hope to be accepted elsewhere.

The two greatest of these city-states were Sparta and Athens, each of which, in its own way, represented an extreme of cultural tradition and social organization within Greek civilization. Other cities at times challenged their supremacy, but none was so powerful or so influential as these two. Sparta, which was early organized into a quasi-military society where the freeborn citizens (Spartiates) controlled a much larger population of noncitizens (perioeci) and slaves (helots), has been the prototype throughout history of the closed, caste-ridden, authoritarian society. Its citizens were devoted to the ideals of self-denial and discipline as laid down in a rigorous code which regulated every aspect of Spartan life. Athens, on the other hand, once it had deposed its hereditary kings age" from which it did not begin to emerge until the evolution of a new language-classical Greek-ushered in the era of true Hillenic civilization about the middle of the eighth century B.C.

2. Homeric Period, c. 850-700 B.C.

Homer's *Iliad* and *Odyssey*, *c.* 850 B.C. Hesiod's poems, *c.* 700 B.C.

3. Early Greek Expansion and Colonization

Asia Minor, *c.* 1100-900 B.C. Sicily and southern Italy (Magna Graecia), *c.* 800-600 B.C. Black Sea (Euxine) area, 756-747 B.C.

4. Sparta

Enslavement of the Messenians made possible the founding of Sparta, *c.* 736-716 B.C. Legendary "Lycurgus the Lawgiver" drew up a severe Spartan social and military code, *c.* 610 B.C. Spartans victorious in Peloponnesian Wars against Athens, 431-404 B.C.

5. Athens

Athenian kingship abolished, *c.* 683 B.C. Legal reforms of Solon instituted, 594 B.C. Athens controlled Delian Confederacy—height of Athenian naval power, 454 B.C. Age of Pericles, 457-429 B.C.

6. Great Age of Hellas, 490-338 B.C.

Joint effort of the Greek city-states defeated the Persians at Marathon (490 B.C.) and Salamis (480 B.C.). Peloponnesian Wars (431-404 B.C.) weakened Greek city-states; Athens never fully recovered from losses. Conquest of Greek city-states by Philip II of Macedon at Battle of Chaeronea (338 B.C.) marked end of Hellenic independence and beginning of Greek absorption into Hellenistic civilization.

7. Major Figures of Greek Civilization

A. PHILOSOPHERS. ■ (1) Sophists, 5th century B.C. Believed that "man is the measure of all things," i.e., that truth is what human beings think it is. This relativist position was attacked by other Greek thinkers who argued that and destroyed the power of its factious nobility, emerged in the 5th century B.C., and particularly in the Age of Pericles (457-429 B.C.), as the classic democracy of the ancient world. By modern standards its democratic practices were extremely limited, since the rights of citizens were not extended to the whole of society. Nevertheless, it offered its people a great measure of opportunity for self-expression and intellectual development which accounts for the great cultural achievements of Athens in the 5th and 4th centuries B.C.

Unhappily for Greek civilization, the polis as a form of government was both its greatest strength and its greatest weakness. Only once in all their history were the city-states of Hellas able to combine successfully against outside danger, and that occurred when the Persian kings, Darius and Xerxes, in successive invasion attempts (490 and 480 B.C.), were defeated by the concerted action of a Hellenic alliance headed by Athens and Sparta. After the final Persian defeat in 479 B.C., incessant rivalry among the city-states, aroused by the growth of Athenian seapower and imperial ambitions, led to a series of internal wars between two alliances under Athenian and Spartan domination. As a consequence of this long struggle, known as the Peloponnesian Wars (431-404 B.C.), Athens was defeated; and though she later recovered some of her former greatness, her position was never so strong again.

The succeeding period from 404 to 323 B.C. was marked by the predominance first of Sparta and then of Thebes. During that time the Persians and later the kings of Macedon (a semibarbarian kingdom to the north) intrigued continuously to keep Hellas disunited. Their success in doing so finally made it possible for King Philip of Macedon (359-336 B.C.) to defeat the Greek city-states one at a time and thus unite all Greece under Macedonian domination. After Philip's death his son, Alexander the Great (336-323 B.C.), embarked with Greek aid on a campaign of conquest which culminated in the destruction of the Persian empire and the formation of a new, short-lived empire stretching from Greece to the borders of India. With Alexander's death in 323 B.C. the classic age of Hellenic civilization reached an end and merged into the Hellenistic, a new and broader civilization that reached far beyond Hellas.

The Greek influence on western civilization has been so great and so significant that no area of western cultural or intellectual activity has been untouched by it. For centuries Greek standards of value in the arts and the characteristic Greek approach to intellectual problems were accepted, almost slavishly, by men who looked backward to the Greeks as beings superior to themselves. Even in our own day, when we have for long rejected some of the specific answers given by the Greeks to the there was an objective, divine knowledge above and beyond man's senses. ■ (2) Socrates, 470?-399 B.C. Native of Athens who, in his search for truth, developed the method known as the "Socratic dialogue," a system of questions and answers intended to make men think about their fundamental beliefs. Socrates concluded that ethics was not a matter of habit but could be deduced rationally, that virtue was knowledge, and that ignorance was the root of moral evil. He was put to death for asking disconcerting questions which his enemies claimed were undermining the morals of Athenian youth. ■ (3) Plato, 427?-347 B.C. Foremost pupil of Socrates, who carried on where his master left off. Believed that men can know the good rationally and that, knowing it, they can also do good. Plato taught that there is an ideal world which exists in perfection above and beyond the material world and that this ideal world, which man knows through his spiritual faculty, is the only real world. ■ (4) Aristotle, 384-322 B.C. Brilliant pupil of Plato and one of the world's great systematizers of human knowledge. Formulated the laws of thought (logic) and tools of intellectual analysis which are the basis of western philosophy. Classified and arranged various fields of knowledge, such as physics, biology, politics. ■

B. ARTISTS. ■ (1) Phidias, 500?-432 B.C. Greatest of Greek sculptors; created the Athena of the Parthenon in Athens and the 40-foot figure of Zeus at Olympia. ■ (2) Praxiteles, 4th century B.C. Creator of the Hellenic masterpiece of sculpture depicting Hermes bearing the infant Dionysius, the only work clearly identified and associated with his name.

C. LITERARY FIGURES. ■ (1) Homer, *c.* 850 B.C. Unknown figure about whom there has always been much speculation. The importance of the *Iliad* and the *Odyssey*, which are attributed to him, is that these two great works had an immense influence on later Greek literature and thought. ■ (2) Hesiod, *c.* 700 B.C. A Boeotian farmer-poet whose chief writings were *Works and Days* and the *Theogony*. The latter work is the chief source for Greek myths and legends about the gods. ■ (3) Pindar, 522?-443 B.C. Theban poet whose lyrics were considered finest after those of Homer. ■ (4) Herodotus, 484?-425 B.C., and Thucydides, *c.* 471-400 B.C. Two historians whose writings are generally conquestions they asked about man and the universe, we must still admit that few have ever formulated those questions more acutely or profoundly than they did.

It was, in fact, the quality of inquisitiveness that made the Greek contribution to western civilization so significant. The Greeks asked questions about almost everything, and they asked them in a very specific way. The Greek was concerned not only to speculate about the gods and man's behavior toward them; he was also concerned with all the complex things (phenomena) of his daily world. Unlike many other ancient peoples, who also developed elaborate systems of philosophy or theology, the Greeks were not content to rely entirely upon the divine, the mysterious, or the unknowable as the means of explaining the world in which they lived. They believed firmly in the power of man's mind to seek out explanations; and they also believed that all the complex, diverse phenomena of the everyday world were governed by underlying harmonious laws which could be fathomed by human reason. This assumption of an underlying order or harmony in nature, while it may have been overstressed by the Greeks, was to have a profound influence on the development of knowledge and thought in mathematics and the natural sciences (astronomy, chemistry, physics), where order and harmony must also be presupposed.

Nor were the Greeks content to deal only with those things which they observed through the senses. They were also curious about man's mental processes and the abstractions which take form as ideas. In their pursuit of philosophy they continually tried to relate ideas to common sense experience, even when, on occasion, their speculations seemed very remote from day-to-day living. The comprehensiveness of their thought and the magnitude of their intellectual achievement, particularly as seen in the writings of the three greatest of their thinkers—Socrates (470?-399 B.C.), Plato (427?-347 B.C.), and Aristotle (384-322 B.C.)—seem all the more remarkable when we remember that for dealing with such problems they had to originate techniques and methods.

In the arts the Greeks were also pioneers. Greek drama was an expression of Greek thought about man and the world. The earliest of the great Hellenic tragedians, Aeschylus (525-456 B.C.) and Sophocles (496?-406 B.C.), presented in their dramas a kind of universal picture of those truths which everyone accepted about mankind and which seemed to demonstrate that there was a moral order in the universe. With the coming of Euripides (480-406 B.C.), the form of the drama changed, for Euripides raised questions about the relations of man with the gods which made it clear that he had serious doubts about the meaning and purpose

sidered the finest examples of Greek prose. Herodotus recounted the history of the Persian Wars and Thucydides
that of the Peloponnesian Wars. ■ (5) Aeschylus, 525-456
B.C. Author of *Prometheus Bound;* deals with the theme of
man's relations with the gods. ■ (6) Aristophanes, *c.* 448-
380 B.C. Master of Greek comedy; author of the *Frogs* and
a number of other plays; harsh social critic whose plays satirized the decline of post-Periclean Athens. ■ (7) Sophocles,
c. 496?-406 B.C. Author of the *Oedipus* trilogy; master of
Greek tragedy; questioned the meaning of life. ■ (8) Euripides, *c.* 480-406 B.C. Author of the *Bacchus, Iphigenia in
Aulis,* and *Madness of Heracles,* in which he raised doubts
about Greek religious belief and the morality of the gods.

8. Summary of the Greek Contribution to Western
Civilization

(1) Quality of inquisitiveness; (2) concern with the
whole of human existence, spiritual as well as material; (3)
belief in the power of the human mind (rationalism) to find
answers to all important questions; (4) belief in the harmony
of the universe.

B. The Hellenistic Age, c. 323-30 B.C.

1. Career of Alexander the Great, 336-323 B.C.

Succeeded his father, Philip II of Macedon, in 336 B.C.;
crushed revolt of Greek city-states, 335; invaded the Persian Empire—battle of Granicus, 334; battle of Issus, 333;
battle of Gaugamela (Arbela), 331; at the death of Darius,
Alexander became Great King of Persia and extended his
conquests to the banks of the Indus River in India.

2. Division of Alexander's Empire, 321-301 B.C.

Ptolemy Soter seized Egypt, 321; civil war (Wars of the
Diadochi) waged among Alexander's generals, 322-301. Battle of Ipsus, 301 B.C., settled final division of Alexander's
kingdom.

3. Hellenistic Age in Greece

Formation of the Aetolian (290 B.C.) and Achaean (280
B.C.) Leagues. Philip V of Macedonia began hostilities with

of the universe as set forth in the older plays. The world, he noted, was not a place where morality inevitably triumphed. In this way, Euripides opened the door to new speculation about the goals of human existence and helped to prepare the way for a fully developed philosophy which, for many Greeks, gradually replaced the older religious faith in the gods. In spite of this great change, the Greeks in their various forms of art never entirely gave up trying to portray certain generalized concepts that were a part of the earlier tradition. Architecture and sculpture, for example, usually demonstrated the harmony of soul and body as well as the Greek notion of balance or moderation in all things *(sophrosyne)*. The most splendid examples of this striving may be seen in the creations of Athenian artists during the 6th and 5th centuries B.C.

B. The Hellenistic Age

This period, which lasted from the death of Alexander until the absorption of the whole eastern Mediterranean into the Roman empire sometime around the beginning of the Christian era, was characterized by (1) the decline of the Greek city-state, (2) the diffusion of Greek culture throughout the ancient world, and (3) the steady progress of Roman conquest.

Following Alexander's death in 323 B.C., the greater part of his vast empire, in the absence of an agreed heir to his power, was fought over (Wars of the Diadochi) and finally divided among his generals. In the early 3rd century B.C. these divisions consisted of Egypt (with Palestine and Phoenicia), ruled by Ptolemy; the former Persian empire, ruled by Seleucus; Macedonia; and the semi-independent Achaean and Aetolian confederacies which comprised the former city-states of Greece. Most of these new states took on the characteristics of despotism as their rulers increasingly claimed for themselves a quasi-divine authority. Successor and fragmented states arose and quarreled. Continuous warfare during the 3rd and 2nd centuries B.C., however, finally brought on Roman inter-

Rome, 215 B.C. Rome made Greek states into dependencies, 146 B.C.

4. Hellenistic Age in Asia

Seleucus I founded Seleucid Empire, 305-280 B.C. Antiochus III defeated by Romans at Magnesia, 190 B.C. Independent kingdom of Pergamum bequeathed to Rome by its last king, 133 B.C. Syria and the remaining lands of the Seleucid Empire made a Roman province, 64 B.C.

5. Hellenistic Age in Egypt

Egypt ruled by the descendants of Ptolemy Soter. Romans intervened (168 B.C.) to save Egypt from conquest by Syria (Seleucid Empire). Egypt became a Roman province at the defeat of Marc Antony and Cleopatra in the battle of Actium, 31 B.C.

6. Cultural Achievements of the Hellenistic Age

A. PHILOSOPHIES. ■ (1) Epicureanism. Founded by Epicurus, an Athenian (342?-270 B.C.), who taught that all of human life was subservient to the pursuit of happiness. He believed, however, that it was best to cultivate the virtues rather than the vices because the latter, if pursued too much, usually caused pain and suffering. Epicurus thought of the universe as consisting of matter made up of atoms; the gods were remote from men; and religion was superstition. His greatest disciple was the Roman philosopher Lucretius (96?-55 B.C.) whose long poem *De Rerum Natura (On the Nature of Things)* set forth the Epicurean philosophy in full. ■ (2) Stoicism. Founded by Zeno of Citium (336-264 B.C.). Though it took various forms, stoicism in general taught that the world was ruled by a divine universal reason in which all mankind shared and that all men were members of a universal brotherhood. The duty of the Stoic was to live according to divine reason and, by cultivating the highest moral virtues, remain indifferent to the external things of this world. Thus he would achieve the true happiness that comes with serenity of mind. ■ (3) Skepticism. Founded by the half-legendary Pyrrho of Elis (360?-270? B.C.). In essence, it was a philosophy that criticized all other philosophies. Skepticism denied that any knowledge was possible because vention in the eastern Mediterranean and thus gradually diminished the independence of the Hellenistic states. By 30 B.C. all had become a part of the Roman empire.

The culture of the Hellenistic age was marked by two tendencies: cosmopolitanism, resulting from the disintegration of the city-state and the diffusion of Greek civilization; and individualism, seemingly caused by the breakdown of older religious loyalties and the disappearance of faith in the polis as the center of all human activity. These developments were accompanied by a growth of trade and finance which enormously increased the wealth of the ancient world. As a result of these changes, new philosophical systems, largely secular in outlook, displaced older modes of thought. Man came to be looked upon as a being essentially interested in the things of this world who needed the guidance of a secularized code of ethics. This guidance the three major philosophical systems of the period (Epicureanism, Stoicism, and Skepticism) sought to give, stressing self-discipline and equanimity in the face of adverse circumstances. Perhaps the greatest achievements of the Hellenistic Age, however, were in the sciences. Euclid and Archimedes in mathematics; Heracleides, Aristarchus, and Hipparchus in astronomy; Eratosthenes in geography; and Herophilus and Erasistratus in medicine, all made contributions of permanent importance in the history of scientific knowledge.

Certain fundamental changes within the Hellenistic world prepared the way for the ultimate absorption of all the states that succeeded the Alexandrian conquest into the Roman system of imperial administration. One important reason for these changes was because the original Greek comminities, while they exported their ideas and culture to Asia and Egypt, were also influenced in their turn by those regions. Throughout the Mediterranean East during the Hellenistic period Greek ways and ideas were accepted and imitated. Upper class Persians, Anatolians, Egyptians assimilated themselves to Greek culture and used the Greek language as a kind of *lingua franca* (universal language) for the conduct of commercial life and administration.

The very success of this Greek cultural expansion, however, had serious consequences for the original communities of the Greek mainland. If the Oriental was increasingly Hellenized, Greece itself was also assimilating Oriental ways. Whatever the reason (and we are still not sure why the change occurred), Greek society, particularly in its economic life, became more and more Oriental in form and structure. The large estate worked by numbers of slaves or wage earning labours displaced the independent small farmer. Cities were populated by a proletariat whose members suffered dreadfully from sudden shifts in economic circumstances.

all sense perceptions are illusions. Therefore, man can know nothing with any certainty. All that he can hope to do is to accept the world as it is and maintain a complete calm in the face of life.

B. SCIENTIFIC ACHIEVEMENTS. ■ (1) Mathematics. Euclid (*c.* 300 B.C.), greatest of Greek geometers, collected all the works of his predecessors and gave to geometry the form which it has taken since. ■ Archimedes of Syracuse (287?-212 B.C.) discovered the idea of specific gravity, worked out the principle of the lever, and found the ratio of the volume of a cylinder to that of a sphere inscribed within it. ■ (2) Astronomy. ■ Heracleides of Pontus (4th century B.C.) about 350 B.C. maintained in his history of astronomy that the earth rotated on its axis and that Venus and Mercury revolved around the sun. ■ Aristarchus of Samos (3rd century B.C.) went further and found by geometry that the sun was larger than the earth; also asserted that the earth moved around the sun. ■ Hipparchus of Nicaea (*c.* 130 B.C.) cleared up the mathematical difficulties in the geocentric (earth-centered) theory of the solar system so that it became the accepted theory until Copernicus disproved it mathematically in the 16th century. ■ (3) Geography. Eratosthenes (3rd century B.C.) calculated the diameter of the earth with a small margin of error; computed the distance from the earth to the sun with an error of only 1%; produced a map with lines of latitude and longitude. ■ (4) Medicine. Herophilus (*c.* 300 B.C.) was the first known to have undertaken anatomical dissection. ■ Erasistratus (*c.* 300 B.C.), pupil of Herophilus, is generally regarded as the founder of physiology.

Even worse, because most of the larger Greek cities depended on food from abroad, any crop failure or interruption of supply could produce serious famines. The result was a continuously growing discontent in most Greek cities which occasionally reached the point of riot or rebellion. Moreover, the growing gap between rich and poor increased class bitterness and further weakened the structure of society.

The great and basic problem of this period, as it was to be of the Roman Empire in its later stages, was that the growth of urbanization had, in many ways, outstripped the technology of the times. The methods of production then available were simply not advanced enough to support the dense city populations of the Hellenistic world. The result was that the insufficiency of wealth produced further tensions by making it very nearly impossible to alleviate the lot of the great mass of the poverty-stricken population.

A further consequence of this situation was the destruction of the old loyalties that had bound the city-state communities of Hellas together. Most Hellenistic cities, therefore, lived in constant danger of social explosion, a situation which, in a measure, must in the end have aided the Roman conquest of the eastern Mediterranean.

To add further to the social difficulties of the Hellenistic world, the traditional religious beliefs no longer appealed to the upper classes. In their place the cultivated rich substituted the secular philosophies mentioned above. These, while satisfactory under normal human conditions, had no great sustaining power in times of crisis. For the masses, on the other hand, a secularized code of ethics was not only remote from their own understanding and experiences but seemed, in fact, only to suggest that they should accept their sufferings with a resigned hopelessness. It is not surprising, therefore, that a whole host of mystery cults should have been recreated (as in the case of the Greek mystery religions) or newly founded. An interesting example of the latter was the worship of Serapis. Serapis, the city god of Alexandria in Egypt, appears to have been a deliberate invention that grew out of a combination of older deities: the Egyptian god Osiris, the Greek Zeus, and the Babylonian Marduk. The cult had the great advantage of offering immortality to those who observed its rituals, a characteristic which may well explain its spread throughout the Hellenistic world.

For all of its extraordinary achievements in science, technology, and the arts, Hellenistic society was slowly losing its creative impulses in the generations just before its conquest by the Romans. The age was one that seems in retrospect to have promised much but which could not continuously sustain the high intellectual and artistic effort of the earlier Hellenic civilization from whence it sprang.

C.   Rome: Republic and Empire, *c.* **509 B.C.-476 A.D.**

1.   The Roman Republic, *c.* 509 B.C.-27 B.C.

A. EARLY HISTORY OF THE CITY. Growth of the power of the masses (plebeians) characterized the early history of Rome. Expulsion of Roman kings, *c.* 509 B.C.   (1) Law of the Twelve Tables formulated as the basis of all later Roman law, 450-449 B.C. Consulship opened to plebeians, 367 B.C.

(2) Reforms of the Gracchi (Tiberius Gracchus, murdered in 133 B.C., and his brother Gaius Gracchus, killed in 121 B.C.) attempted to redistribute land and wealth in favor of the Roman masses.

B. CIVIL WARS OF THE 1ST CENTURY B.C. Internal disturbances led to a series of dictatorships, sometimes favoring the aristocracy and sometimes the plebeians. Despite efforts of various powerful leaders—Marius, Sulla, Pompey, and, finally, Julius Caesar—to restore order, none could do so successfully until Octavius (Augustus) Caesar suppressed the warring factions and seized power in 27 B.C. By this action the Roman Republic ceased to exist and was gradually transformed into a centralized empire.

C. EXPANSION OF THE ROMAN REPUBLIC, 338-31 B.C. Rome defeated Latin League, 338 B.C.; conquered the Samnites, 327-290 B.C.; defeated Pyrrhus of Epirus and seized Magna Graecia (southern Italy), 281-272 B.C. First Punic War with Carthage, 264-241 B.C. Sicily, Sardinia, and Corsica became first Roman provinces, 227 B.C. Second Punic War, 218-201 B.C., ended after defeat of Hannibal by the Roman general Scipio Africanus at the battle of Zama (Africa), 202 B.C. Third Punic War, 149-146 B.C., led to the ruthless destruction of Carthage. Macedonia became a Roman province, 146 B.C. Conquest and reorganization of Asia by Pompey, 66-62 B.C. Caesar's conquest of Gaul, 58-51 B.C. Egypt became a Roman province, 31 B.C.

2.   The Roman Empire, 27 B.C.-476 A.D.

A. THE EARLY EMPIRE, 27 B.C.-180 A.D. Augustus Caesar granted imperial power for life, 23 B.C. Roman armies defeated by Germans under Varus (battle of Teutoburger Forest), 9 A.D. Imperial expansion continued under Tiberius,

C. Rome: Republic and Empire

From the point of view of western man, ancient history culminates with the absorption of the whole Mediterranean basin into the single great politial entity known as the Roman Empire. The history of this great empire, which so influenced world history, divides into two obvious parts. The first period, that of the Roman republic, lasted from about 509 B.C., when the Romans expelled the last of their early kings, to 27 B.C. when Augustus (27 B.C.-14 A.D.) emerged as the first Roman emperor. The second, or imperial, period extended from the reign of Augustus to the end of the Roman Empire in the West toward the end of the 5th century A.D.

The story of Rome is one of a fairly steady and almost uninterrupted expansion during which a small hill town near the mouth of the Tiber River in west central Italy became the great urban center of a vast empire which encircled the Mediterranean and ultimately included all or parts of modern England, France, Germany, and Spain. This growth was not the result of any carefully conceived plan but of a need, first, to defend the city itself and then, later, to protect the distant frontiers of regions which Roman conquest had added over a long period of time. In this fashion, Roman conquests compounded themselves; for, as the territories of Rome grew, other, more distant, peoples continually threatened Roman security. In the end, this continuous expansion forced the city to become an imperial power and drove the Romans to change their quasi-democratic republican institutions in order to set up a system of government which could more effectively deal with the complex administrative problems of a great empire.

In its early stages (before 31 B.C.), this expansion was marked by several important wars of survival and conquest. Defeating first their immediate neighbors the Etruscans, the Romans gradually extended their territory until by 265 B.C. all Italy was conquered. With Italy secured, Rome then found herself involved in a series of fateful wars with the North African state of Carthage. In three separate struggles known as the Punic Wars (264-241 B.C., 218-202 B.C., and 149-146 B.C.), Rome destroyed Carthage completely and converted Carthaginian territories into Roman provinces. During the second of these wars Rome first turned her attention to the East, where Philip V, king of Macedonia, had allied himself with the famous Carthaginian general Hannibal and started to war against Rome, setting in motion the train of events leading to Roman conquest of Greece and the Near East.

With the last of these conquests Rome herself began to change. Grad-

14-37 A.D., Caligula, 37-41 A.D., Claudius, 41-54 A.D. (under whom Romans began conquest of British in 43 A.D.), and Nero, 54-68 A.D. Empire reached its greatest extent under the "five good emperors": Nerva, 96-98 A.D., Trajan, 98-117 A.D., Hadrian, 117-138 A.D., Antoninus Pius, 138-161 A.D., and Marcus Aurelius (whose *Meditations* made him famous also as a philosopher), 161-180 A.D.

B. THE LATER EMPIRE, 180-476 A.D. After 180 A.D. the forces of disintegration were clearly at work. The empire was increasingly controlled by military factions who deposed and often murdered emperors. The state was no longer able to maintain its extended frontiers or to preserve internal order. Gradually, the machinery of government ceased to function with its former effectiveness. Taxes became more difficult to collect, and the productive capacity of the empire declined. "Barrack emperors" ruled the empire with the support of the army, 235-284. Two emperors appointed to rule, 293.

Growing Christian minority persecuted, 303-311. Empire divided under eastern and western emperors, 305; permanent division of the empire began. Imperial order gave to Christianity equal rights with all other religions of the empire, 313. Founding of Constantinople as capital of Eastern Empire by Emperor Constantine, 330. Conversion to Christianity and death of Constantine, 337. Invading Goths defeated imperial armies at Adrianople, 378. Sack of Rome by Alaric and the Visigoths, 410. Romans defeated the invading Huns under Attila at the battle of Chalons, 451. Sack of Rome by Gaeseric and the Vandals, 455. Odoacer, a Latinized German in command of the Roman armies, deposed the last western emperor (Romulus Augustulus) and ruled as a separate, independent king in Italy, 476.

3. Major Figures of Roman Civilization

A. STATESMEN AND MILITARY LEADERS. (1) Scipio Africanus, 237-183 B.C. Defeated Hannibal and the Carthaginian army at the battle of Zama (Africa), 202 B.C. (2) Marcus Porcius Cato ("the Censor"), 234-149 B.C. Roman senator and chief of the landowning party who demanded the destruction of Carthage in the Third Punic War by insisting "delenda est Carthago" (Carthage must be destroyed). (3) Gnaeus Pompey, 106-48 B.C. Conqueror of Syria

ually the city expanded in wealth and population until it became a huge
dependent urban growth whose subsistence was derived from outlying
areas and whose social structure was altered in such a way as to create
tensions among the various classes. During most of the 1st century B.C.
Rome was torn by civil wars and social strife which usually centered round
the dictatorial chiefs of powerful factions. The greatest of these was
Julius Caesar, who was murdered by his political enemies in 44 B.C. In
the end, it was a young relative of Caesar's, Octavian (Augustus), who
restored order by suppressing the various warring elements and making
himself the first of the Roman emperors.

Under Augustus and his successors, imperial Rome reached the peak
of its wealth and greatness as the central power of the state was increasingly consolidated around the person of the emperor and as the boundaries
of the empire were steadily expanded. By 117 A.D. the empire reached
its broadest extent, but even as it grew there were already signs of decay.
The cost of maintaining large military forces, the continuing economic
dependence of the capital city upon the provinces, the increasing insecur-
ity of the emperors, who depended more and more upon the army to
keep them in power, the inability of the empire to absorb large numbers
of infiltrating barbarians, all helped to weaken the central authority and
undermine the social structure. In their desperation the later emperors
resorted to repressive measures in the form of harsh taxation and economic
regulation that slowly strangled economic activity and thus further compounded the difficulties of the state. Meanwhile, Christianity, which had
been introduced into Rome from the Near East during the 1st century
A.D., gradually spread throughout the empire. At the opening of the 4th
century (*c.* 313) it was granted equal status with the older pagan religions
on orders of the emperor Constantine. In the end, the various forces of
disintegration led to the deposition of the last western emperor (as distinct from the eastern emperor who, after the division of the empire into
two parts in 395, ruled the eastern half from Constantinople) and his
replacement by a barbarian king. With this symbolic event the real unity
of the Roman empire was destroyed. In its place appeared the numerous
German tribal principalities which became the bases of modern European
nationhood.

The most important contribution of the Roman world to later western history is to be found in its bringing together of the various streams
of ancient civilization and its transmission of these to the European successor states. Though the Romans added to Greek thought little that was
original (they were particularly deficient in science and philosophy), they
were enough impressed by it to act as its disseminators. For the spread

and Roman Asia; ruled Rome as a part of a triumvirate (three-man dictatorship) with Crassus and Julius Caesar (who was his son-in-law); became sole dictator in 52 B.C. and was finally defeated by Julius Caesar at the battle of Pharsalus, 48 B.C. ■ (4) Julius Caesar, *c.* 100-44 B. C. Conqueror of Gaul; member of triumvirate with Pompey; after his victory at Pharsalus became virtually an absolute dictator. From fear that he was about to establish some kind of permanent monarchy, he was assassinated by a band of plotters led by Marcus Junius Brutus in 44 B.C. ■ (5) Marcus Antonius (Marc Antony), *c.* 83-30 B.C. Associate of Julius Caesar who later divided power with Octavius (Augustus) Caesar. He fell under the influence of and later married Cleopatra of Egypt. When he tried to dispose of Rome's eastern provinces in her favor, he was defeated by Augustus at Actium in 31 B.C. and afterwards took his own life. ■ (6) Augustus Caesar (Octavius or Octavianus), 63 B.C.-14 A.D. Greatnephew and adopted heir of Julius Caesar; restored order in Roman provinces and became first Roman emperor (princeps), 27 B.C.-14 A.D. ◙ (7) Trajan (Marcus Ulpius Traianus), *c.* 52-117 A.D. Usually thought of as the greatest emperor after Augustus; excellent soldier; able administrator; expanded the empire to its greatest territorial extent; ruled from 98 to 117 A.C. ■ (8) Marcus Aurelius (Antonius), 121-180 A.D. Last of the "five good emperors'; able soldier and administrator; preserved the empire from invasion; Stoic philosopher whose *Meditations* have a Christian flavor. ■ (9) Diocletian, 245-313 A.D. Emperor who restored order after a period of anarchy ("crisis of the third century") and instituted a series of reforms which, for a time, stopped the decay of the Roman state. Remembered for his persecution of Christians. Came to the throne in 284; abdicated in 305. ■ (10) Constantine the Great, 280?-337 A.D. Successor of Diocletian; established Christianity on equal footing with other religions and later made it the state religion; converted the empire into a hereditary monarchy. Ruled from 305 to 337. ■ (11) Justinian, 483-565 A.D. Emperor of the East (527-565) who almost succeeded in reunifying the eastern and western halves of the empire by conquest. His most enduring work was the collection and condification of the Roman law which has come down in history as the Code of Justinian.

of Christianity they provided a stable political setting and an institutional framework which was copied by the Christian church and enabled the church to grow in strength through the centuries. To the world of European literature and thought the Romans bequeathed their Latin language, which was to become an influential element in the formation of almost every western European tongue. Of equal importance were Rome's laws and her system of universal government, from both of which many of the later political institutions of Europe were derived.

Historical Problem of Rome's Decline. The reason for the long decline and ultimate disappearance of the Roman empire of the West has long stirred the imagination of historians. In part, the continuing interest in the "decline and fall" of Rome stems from the fact that historians are always curious about the reasons why any great civilization disappears into oblivion. In the case of the western Roman Empire, however, curiosity is compounded by the fact that the empire lasted for so many centuries and seemed, both to contemporaries and to later generations, to be one of the most stable and longest-lived political entities ever created. Its disintegration, therefore, seemed to those who witnessed the last days of the Roman Empire to be the end of the world. Indeed, it was this very sense of secular hopelessness that the great Christian thinker, Augustine (356–430), sought to combat in a famous work entitled *The City of God.* Augustine argued that while the "City of Man", i.e. Rome, might well fade from history, men should still be of good hope. The "City of God", i.e. Christianity, would take its place, and men might, therefore, be consoled by the hope of a kingdom that was not of this world.

Nevertheless, though the views of Augustine and other Christian theologians, offered consolation to faithful Christian believers, other Romans thought the decline of the empire a disaster and undertook to explain it in various ways. Even so early as the end of the first century A.D. the Roman historian, Tacitus (*c.* 55–*c.*117 A.D.), suggested that the decline of older republican virtues, particularly in the army, led to a moral decay which rotted the empire from within. Some emperors of the third and fourth centuries, most notably Julian the Apostate, who ruled from 361 to 363, tried to restore the old pagan religion in the hope that this might revive the ancient virtues.

Much later in European history historians came to share a widely held view that the Roman Empire was destroyed by invading hordes of barbarians (Huns, Ostrogoths, Visigoths, Vandals) who poured over the imperial frontiers in such numbers that they could not be resisted. The flood of these uncivilized warriors was so great, they believed, that it inundated Roman civilization and ushered in the long period known as

B. MAJOR FIGURES OF ROMAN CULTURE. (1) Cicero, 106-43 B.C. Greatest of Roman rhetoricians (orators), whose speeches and writings proved him one of the great masters of the Latin language. (2) The Roman Historians. Livy, 59 B.C.-17 A.D., in his *History of Rome* described the beginnings of the city and the origins of Roman greatness to a later generation. Tacitus, 55?- after 117 A.D., in his *Annals* and *Histories,* strove to demonstrate to the Romans of his day how decadent they had become. (3) Vergil (or Virgil), 70-19 B.C. Greatest Roman epic poet; author of the *Aeneid,* which tells at length the story of Rome's founding by the legendary Aeneas of Troy. (4) Ovid, 43 B.C.-17 A.D.? Author of a handbook of Greek mythology known as the *Metamorphoses* and numerous witty poems. (5) Two Roman Satirists. Satire in its pure form was an original contribution of the Romans to western literature. Its first major practitioner was Horace, 65-8 B.C., whose *Odes* made him the second greatest of the Latin poets (after Vergil). The greatest of Roman satirists, however, was Juvenal, 60?-140? A.D., whose *Satires* still give a harsh but shrewd and subtle picture of Roman life.

4. Summary of the Roman Contribution to Western Civilization

(1) Transmission of the traditions and learning of the ancient world; (2) stable political framework for the growth of Christianity; (3) Latin language and literature; (4) Roman law and government.

"the Dark Ages" from which Europe did not begin to recover for almost a thousand years. The great shortcoming of this overly simple explanation, however, was that it overlooked one very important consideration. Rome had been threatened by outside enemies time after time throughout its history. On countless previous occasions, Roman armies had thrown the invaders back or conquered and enslaved them.

Why were the Romans of the later period (4th and 5th centuries) unable to do what Romans of earlier periods had done so often and so effectively? The answer to this question began to be pondered by historians from about the eighteenth century onward. One of the first modern historians to think about this question at length was the great British scholar, Edward Gibbon (1737-1794), whose many-volumed *Decline and Fall of the Roman Empire* remains one of the classics of historical writing even to this day. Gibbon concluded that if the later Romans were unable to resist barbarian incursions, it was not because the barbarians were numerically stronger or more warlike than earlier invaders. On the contrary, it seemed obvious to Gibbon, as it had to some Roman observers, that something had happened to the Romans themselves which made them less successful in resisting outside assault. Gibbon implied that a partial explanation might be found in the emergence of Christianity which weakened the warlike spirit of the Romans.

Gibbon's views in this connection are no longer widely accepted by scholars. Nevertheless, most contemporary historians would agree that the "fall of the Roman Empire" came about as a result of internal causes. At present, while there is still a great deal of varied scholarly opinion on the subject, the most widely held views might be summarized as follows: (1) the empire collapsed for a combination of economic and social reasons; (2) the most important of these was growth of the city of Rome whose huge population had to be supported at the expense of the provinces; and (3) by the failure of the empire to improve its (technological) productive capacities above the level of a slave economy.

CHAPTER 5

The Making of
Europe, 5.00-1000

THE ESSENTIAL MOVEMENT

In modern times it has been customary to think of Europe as a separate geographic entity, a continent distinct from the other continental land masses of the earth. This is an anomaly, for Europe is not geographically but culturally separated from Asia and Africa; and even in cultural terms it is not always easy to determine Europe's boundaries since so much of European civilization has been derived from or overlapped into Asia and Africa. For purposes of definition most historians now think of Europe as the creation of a Latin western culture fostered and spread by the medieval Latin church. In this sense Europe does possess a measure of cultural unity which, in all its essentials, was formed in the period extending from the end of the 5th century A.D. to the beginning of the 11th century A.D. The three prominent characteristics of this period are: (1) the superseding of the urban civilization of Rome by an agrarian society whose economic structure was based upon the great estate or manor and whose political organization was determined by the personal-contractual relations of feudalism; (2) the development of the western church under the headship of the Roman pontiff (pope) to a point where, in the 12th and 13th centuries, it became a supranational institution of great moral power and authority; and (3) the beginnings of a conception of unified political authority under the rule of

EVENTS AND DEFINITIONS

A. The Christian Foundations

1. The Origins of Christianity

A. GREEK SOURCES. Decline of the traditional Greek religions during the Hellenistic Age left many Greeks without any belief that transcended their daily lives. Secular or vaguely religious philosophies like Epicureanism, Stoicism, or Skepticism were not enough to fill the void, particularly among the masses. Thus there occurred during the period of Roman rule a gradual revival of interest in religion and religious ceremonies, especially in those originating in the Orient. Of these eastern religions, one was Christianity, which soon transcended all others in importance and began to spread rapidly through the Greek portions of the empire from the end of the 1st century A.D.

B. JEWISH SOURCES. Growth of a strong and traditional Messianic feeling (belief in the imminent coming of a Messiah or savior) among the Jews of the 1st century B.C. and the later infiltration of Greek ideas into Jewish thought prepared the way for the acceptance of Christianity.

C. LIFE OF CHRIST. Recounted in the four gospels according to Matthew, Mark, Luke, and John. Birth of Jesus Christ at Bethlehem in Judaea, c. 4 B.C. Mission and preaching of Christ, c. 26-30 A.D. Crucifixion, c. 30 A.D.

D. TEACHINGS OF JESUS CHRIST. It should be remembered that an important part of the teaching of Jesus was through the example of his own life, since his acts as well as his words had a great impact on those who knew him or were told about him. In the main, his teachings were simple: true religion comes from the heart; and all the law and the prophets' teachings depend on two commandments—love God and love thy neighbor.

E. UNIVERSALITY OF CHRISTIAN APPEAL. What was important in these teachings, however, was that they appealed to all men, whatever their stations in life, and more particularly to the mass of lowly and humble persons throughout the empire. Moreover, Christianity in its primitive form offered a hope to those whose lot in life was an unhappy one.

the feudal king which, in time, was to lead to the development of the modern national state.

A. The Christian Foundations

It is important to remember that medieval civilization was profoundly Christian in the sense that Christian beliefs and standards, though sometimes imperfectly realized, were the bases of thought and the molders of tradition. Christ was the divine redeemer of mankind who had provided the means by which all men, whatever their race or social condition, might hope to achieve a life immortal. In the view of medieval man, the means of attaining this end had been given by Christ to his apostles and thus to the Christian church. Hence the church's duty was to preserve the faith and orthodoxy of those who already believed and to strive to win over those who did not. This strong sense of obligation, which was first put into practice by St. Paul, the "apostle to the gentiles," in the 1st century A.D., made Christianity a powerful missionary religion and led during the early middle ages (6th through 10th centuries) to its expansion into northern and western Europe. As its missionaries spread the faith, the church everywhere adapted itself to a variety of social conditions and imparted through its institutions not only the ethics and beliefs of Christianity but also certain of the traditions of classical antiquity which had been made a part of Christian teaching by the fathers of the church. Apart, however, from its ethical and cultural influences, the Latin church also had an important secular effect on the life of medieval man. Through the machinery of an international bureaucracy and by its dissemination of the Roman law, the church became the teacher of the feudal monarchies, which quickly adapted the practices of ecclesiastical administration to serve their own ends. By means, too, of the great monastic orders (originating in the East but transferred to the West by Benedict of Nursia in the 6th century), techniques and skills of various kinds were developed and spread through societies where they would otherwise have been unknown. The medieval Latin church thus evolved into a massive international organization whose spiritual head, the pope, possessed enormous temporal as well as ecclesiastical power.

Perhaps more important for the larger development of western civilization, however, was the body of practices and ideas that came into being within the community of western Latin Christianity, i.e., that body of Christian communicants who over the centuries looked to the Roman pontiffs for spiritual leadership. The Latin Christian tradition was, indeed, to be of such significance in the development of later western civilization that

2.   The Spread of Christianity

The appeal of Christian teaching and the story of Christ's resurrection quickly gave the new religion a following among the Jews, but it was not until the conversion of the Hellenized Jew, Saul of Tarsus (afterwards known to Christians as St. Paul), that Christianity began to win converts extensively outside Judaic circles.

A. WORK OF PAUL, C. 34-60 A.D. Paul, a Roman citizen and learned in the Greek language and literature, was able to speak to the Roman world in a widely understood tongue; and he also elaborated the first Christian theology in attempting to explain the new faith. Paul pressed the view that non-Jews (gentiles) need not become Jews or observe the Hebraic religious laws in order to become Christians but needed only to have faith in Christ. In this way Christianity ceased to be a sect of Judaism and became a separate universal religion.

B. CHRISTIANIZATION OF THE ROMAN EMPIRE, 64-455 A.D. Fire of Rome—massacre of Christians under Nero, 64 A.D. Rescript of Marcus Aurelius against Christians, 169. Persecutions of the Emperor Decius, 249-251. General toleration granted to Christians by Constantine and the Eastern Emperor Licinius ("Edict of Milan"), 313. Council of Nicaea defined the doctrine of the trinity for orthodox Christian belief, 325. Conversion and death of Constantine, 337. Western bishops were subjugated to Pope Leo I by order of Emperor Valentinian III (supremacy of Roman bishops), 455.

C. RISE OF MONASTICISM AND THE SPREAD OF CHRISTIANITY TO NORTHERN AND WESTERN EUROPE, C. 360-1000. ■ (1) Monasticism, the ascetic practice of living apart from the world of men, did not originate with Christianity but came to be associated with it at a very early period in the Christian communities of Syria and Egypt where it was well established in the 3rd and 4th centuries. It was carried to the West about the middle of the 4th century and there was given the form of a corporate community (all monks lived together in a monastery) by St. Benedict of Nursia in 529. According to St. Benedict's rule (on which all later monastic rules were founded), it was the monk's duty to do the "work of God"—praying, fasting, performing the rites of the church, working with his hands (and, later, with his brains). Traveling as lone missionaries or in groups, it would be impossible to enumerate all or even most of its major contributions in brief space. Nevertheless, some are of such transcendent importance that they must be mentioned here.

Even as the Roman Empire itself had been the means by which much of the civilization of antiquity was transmitted to Europe and the West, so too was Latin Christianity. The Latin Church was, after all, an institutional creation of the late Roman Empire. The center of its administrative authority was at Rome, and the Roman bishops, from a very early period, were generally acknowledged as heads of the church. Furthermore, the diocesan centers of ecclesiastical administration were usually situated in older centers of Roman imperial administration. This meant that even when the empire itself had disappeared, the outline of its defunct system of government was preserved in the organization of the church itself. Thus it was that the church continued to hope for a restoration of that last imperial system which had nurtured it in its beginnings, and to strive throughout the early middle ages for a revival of strong Roman rule.

But more, the church also kept alive the language of the empire. The Latin tonque, though it gradually underwent transformation during the immediate past-Roman and later medieval periods, remained the liturgical language which every cleric had to have some knowledge of in order to perform his ecclesiastical functions. In this way, as the church's influence spread into the remotest corners of Europe, later generations were provided with a key which unlocked for them some part at least of the great artistic and intellectual treasury of classical civilization.

A continuing knowledge of the secular intellectual tradition of antiquity created a curious problem for Christianity, however, which was not finally to be resolved until the high middle ages. Early Christians were singularly indifferent to things of this world, including secular learning. They were convinced, first of all, that they were only sojourners in this world. Christ had seemed to imply in His conversations with His disciples that He would soon return to this earth and that this second coming would usher in the last days foretold by prophecy. Buoyed by this hope of imminent return, the earliest Christians tended to believe that any plans for the permanent existence of a Christian community in a secular would were vain and needless. As time passed, however, and the second coming became an ever remoter hope, the practices and attitudes of Christians began to change in two significant ways.

First, in order to preserve orthodoxy and to keep in communication with the ever-spreading branches of the Christian community, the church ceased to be a loose confederation of congregations and become an organically organized institution. With this transformation the early church be-the Christian monks of the early middle ages were important in the spread of Christianity throughout the north and west of Europe. ■ (2) Spread of Christianity to Northern and Western Europe. St. Patrick's mission to Ireland, *c.* 431; beginning of a separate Celtic church. St. Columba, an Irish monk, carried Christianity into Scotland, 563. St. Augustine of Canterbury reintroduced Christianity into England, 597. Irish (Celtic) church submitted to the Latin Catholic (Roman) church at Synod of Whitby, 664. Mission of the English monk, St. Boniface (Winfred), established the Latin church in Germany, 722-754. Conversion of Scandinavia (Denmark, Norway, Sweden), *c.* 950-1000.

3. The Development of Christian Theology: the Early Fathers

As Christianity spread, it was confronted with the serious problem of determining what was the true or orthodox belief of Christians, particularly in view of the large number of variant interpretations given to Christ's teachings. One of the ways in which the early church dealt with this problem was by summoning great councils, like the Council of Nicaea (see p. 56) which defined orthodox belief on the nature of the trinity in the Nicene creed. With their increasing authority over the whole church, the Roman bishops (popes) successfully asserted their claim to adjudicate in matters of heresy; and councils were called with less frequency until they finally fell into abeyance. During these early centuries, however, the orthodox theology which both popes and councils preached was defined by a number of theologians who came to be known as "Fathers of the Church." Among the more famous of these fathers were those listed below.

A. ATHANASIUS, 293?-373. Saint and bishop of Alexandria who attacked the Arian heresy (see p. 60) by asserting the unity of God and the divinity of Christ.

B. JEROME, 340?-420. Translated the Bible from Greek and Hebrew sources into the Latin Vulgate edition which became the standard for the western church.

C. JOHN CHRYSOSTOM, 345?-407. Saint and patriarch of Constantinople (398-404); most influential of the Greek fathers; elevated asceticism in Christian practice and stressed the importance of scriptural study.

gan a pattern of development which later saw Christianity evolve into the most highly institutionalized of all the world's great religions. The growth of this institutionalization was unquestionably of enormous importance for later periods of European and western history. Not only did this development lead to the creation of one of the greatest supranational institutions the world has ever seen, namely, the medieval church, but it also provided for the continuous acquisition and augmentation of a body of administrative experience which later enabled the church to act as the teacher of the medieval monarchy. In the ultimate, then, it may be said that the church's institutional administrative experience contributed significantly to the formation of that other unique institutional creation of the western world, the modern national state.

Second, once it was plain that Christianity would have to exist in the secular historical world for an unforeseeably long time, the church had to come to grips with certain of the secular intellectual influences by which it was surrounded. It was all well and good for ascetic Christians to preach that secular learning and philosophy were irrelevancies with which no true believer firmly fixed upon otherworldly goals should concern himself. The writings and the philosophical speculation of the great pagans existed and could not be completely ignored. Indeed, as time passed and more and more intellectuals in late Roman society became Christian converts, it was virtually impossible for these men to completely forget the intellectual baggage they had accumulated before embracing the new faith. St. Augustine of Hippo is an excellent case in point. Augustine as a young man had been schooled in the pagan philosophies. When he became a Christian, he accepted the common Christian view that his earlier intellectual training was irrelevant to his new found Christian aspirations. And yet he could not cast aside this knowledge or the ways of thought imparted by his pagan teachers. As he speculated about the relationship between the human and the divine, about God's grace and man's will, he inevitably used the familiar modes of thought. In brief, he speculated rationally on these matters even though he did not believe that reason alone could lead to faith. The important thing about him and generations of Christian thinkers like him was that they were creating that highly rationalized, highly sophisticated body of religious thought which we know as theology. Time after time in the history of the Christian church theologians might protest that their speculations were vain; that men could never hope to come to a knowledge of God through reason alone. And yet they continually yielded to intellectual temptation. Thus, by a kind of paradox, Christianity tended to preserve, almost against its will, ways of thinking that had come into existence with the Greeks and thus helped, inadvertently, to carry the Hellenic tra-

D. AUGUSTINE, 354-430. Saint and bishop of Hippo in North Africa; greatest of the Latin (western) fathers. Attacked the Pelagian or free-will heresy (see below) and laid stress on justification by faith. Prepared the way for the acceptance of Christian theology by the Germanic peoples of northern Europe. Augustine was a dominant force in Latin (western) theology throughout the early middle ages.

4. Heresies

The following were some of the more troublesome of the heresies that divided the early church.

A. ARIANISM. Formulated by Arius of Alexandria early in the 4th century, it tried to explain the relationship between Father and Son in the trinity by saying that Christ, though possessing divine substance, was not co-equal with God. This teaching was condemned by the Council of Nicaea in 325 but persisted for some generations thereafter.

B. GNOSTICISM. Belief that knowledge (*gnosis*) will liberate one from the physical (material) world, which is deemed not real but only an illusion, the real world being that of the spirit.

C. PELAGIANISM. Named for the 4th-century British monk Pelagius, this doctrine argued that men were free of original sin and had control of their own moral destinies (free will). Condemned by Augustine and others because it lessened the divine power of God.

D. NESTORIANISM. Belief taught by Bishop Nestorius in the early 5th century to the effect that Christ was in two harmonious but distinct natures, human and divine. This belief led to a denial of the motherhood of the Virgin Mary and was condemned by the Council of Ephesus in 431.

E. MONOPHYSITISM. Belief that grew up, particularly in Syrian and Egyptian Christianity, that Christ was of one composite nature (not two as the Nestorians had taught) which was both human and divine. Its condemnation as a heresy by the Council of Chalcedon in 451 so angered its Syrian and Egyptian supporters that they later offered little resistance to Islamic (Mohammedan) conquest.

dition of rationality over into western thought. In this respect, as in its institutionalization, Christianity made a unique contribution to the development of the western tradition. Other great religions approached this sophisticated level of theological speculation for longer or short periods of time but none continued the practice so consistently over so many centuries. If this strange circumstance had not occurred, it is hard to imagine how the later western intellectual tradition could have come into being.

And, finally, we must remember that if Christianity inadvertently, indeed almost accidently, kept alive the Greek ways of rational thinking, it more consciously preserved the outlook of another ancient people. Christianity extended forward in time certain of the uniquely significant assumptions about God, man, and history first enunciated by the prophets of Israel. History was not purposeless in the Christian view. It moved toward a rendezvous at the end of time. No event, therefore, was ever meaningless or random. It was always a part of God's divine plan for the world. Moreover, men knew how they were expected to participate in this plan. They were expected to obey the ethical injunctions of God. In this way the western tradition was infused and informed by a set of moral assumptions, which, though often imperfectly realized, later guided much of western social and political development.

B.   Germanic Influences: the Rise of Feudalism

1.   Germanic Invasions

A. VANDALS, 406-548. Entered Gaul, 406; crossed into Spain (409) and Africa (429) where they established a kingdom that lasted until 534 when it was finally conquered by the Emperor Justinian.

B. OSTROGOTHS (EAST GOTHS). Invasion of Italy by Theodoric the Ostrogoth, 488; establishment of Ostrogothic kingdom of Italy, 493-535. Reconquest of Italy by Justinian, 535-554.

C. VISIGOTHS (WEST GOTHS) invaded Spain, 415. Visigothic kingdom of Spain established, 466-711. Conversion of Visigoths to Latin Christianity, 587. Beginning of Islamic conquest of Spain (battle of Guadalete), 711.

D. LOMBARDS invaded Italy, 568; conquered northern and central areas, 568-605. Converted to Latin Christianity, *c.* 650. Lombard kingdom absorbed into the Frankish empire of Charlemagne, 774.

E. FRANKS penetrated into Gaul at the end of the 4th century. Consolidation of the Frankish kingdom under Clovis, 481-511. Merovingian kingdom of the Franks taken over by the descendants of Charles Martel (481-754). Pepin the Short crowned king of the Franks, 754. Charlemagne (Charles the Great) ruled as king of the Franks, 768-814, and as Roman Emperor of the West, 800-814.

F. THE ANGLO-SAXONS. Roman legions withdrawn from Britain, 407-422. Angles, Saxons, and Jutes invaded England from the European continent, *c.* 450-615. Anglo-Saxon heptarchy (seven small kingdoms) united under Alfred the Great (871-879), king of Wessex, and his two sons, Edward (899-924) and Athelstane (924-939).

2.   Manorialism

The "manor" or estate was the economic and social unit of medieval life. Like a modern farm, it varied in size from a few to many thousands of acres. It was the manor, worked by serfs or tenants of its lord or holder, that provided subsistence

B. Germanic Influences: the Rise of Feudalism

With the disappearance of Rome's centralized authority in the 5th century and the emergence of the Germanic successor kingdoms, the society of the old west Roman provinces began to change. In part, this transformation was the result of a decline in city life, outside Italy in particular, and the disappearance of the forms of economic organization which had made possible the existence of the highly centralized, bureaucratic Roman state. Necessity thus drove the inhabitants of the empire to localize their government and other institutions in order to secure themselves against attack and to become economically self-sufficient. The customary unit of such organization was the great estate (manor), whose owner became the patron of a large number of dependents, from whom he received labor in return for protection and food.

As the Germanic tribes moved into the empire, this system was slowly fused with the Germanic tribal custom by which the members of a tribal war band bound themselves in an oath of loyalty to their chief. From these two distinct Roman and German sources there evolved the later system of social organization usually described as feudalism. Under feudalism the basic economic and political unit was the manorial estate which provided society with subsistence and military power. Social relationships between lord and vassal were governed by the feudal contract which laid down the reciprocal obligations from one to the other. In modern times it has been customary to regard feudalism as a repressive and dangerously decentralizing form of social and political organization. It should be remembered, however, that in spite of its shortcomings in modern eyes, it was the only means of providing security and social stability over fairly wide areas in societies that were predominantly agricultural.

The feudal-manorial system in its fully developed form, however, was not to be reached until later in the middle ages. In the period between the fifth and seventh centuries it had not yet come into being in the strictest sense, for this was the time when the Germanic invaders of empire were only beginning to establish themselves in regions which would later become the feudal kingdoms of the high middle ages and, at a more remote date, the national monarchies of early modern Europe. To a large extent, it may in fact be said that historical chance determined these later developments, for the original regions where these Germanic tribes settled were where they happened to find themselves by luck or conquest at a particular moment in historic time.

for feudal society. Most of those who worked the manor were serfs or "unfree" men (they were not slaves in the sense that their bodies were owned by a master, since they could not be removed from the manor) bound to the manor and obligated to furnish uncompensated labor on the lord's lands as well as a portion of their own crops. The lord himself was usually not the outright owner of his manor in the modern sense but held it under the authority of someone else for whom he was obligated to do certain services. For the lord, however, and those like him higher up the feudal social ladder, this relationship, unlike that between the serf and the lord of the manor, was not servile but honorable under terms of the feudal contract (see below).

3.   Feudalism and the Feudal Contract

Feudalism was a set of contractural arrangements under which most of feudal society was governed. As a system of government, it was neither inherently evil nor inferior to other systems. In a sense, it was simply a necessary means of operating an agricultural society which had no strong centralized government and had to protect itself against invasion and preserve the stability of its social relations and institutions. The binding element of feudal society, therefore, was the feudal contract between lords and vassals who made up the ruling nonservile classes of that society (serfs or unfree men were not a part of the feudal contract). By entering into this contract (in which the vassal formally acknowledged the suzerain as his overlord and did homage for his land), the suzerain (or higher lord) was assured that the vassal (or lesser lord) would undertake to furnish his feudal superior certain services, usually of a military nature, while the vassal was assured of protection in return. In order to make the system work, the vassal had to have land for his own subsistence and the subsistence of those dependent upon him and to provide the services for which he was obligated to the suzerain. Thus it was that landholding and the obligations attached to it were absolutely essential to the existence of feudalism and determined a man's social as well as his economic position in society.

Who were the Germans? Their origins are obscure, but from what we can determine from archeological evidence they appear to have been one of several waves of invaders who began to move outward from Scandinavia sometime about 1000 B.C. If the evidence is correct it would thus appear that they were related ethnically to the later Vikings (see pp. 70-71). Historians have long puzzled over the reasons why this movement, known commonly by the German word *Völkerwänderungen* (wanderings of the peoples) should have occurred. At present we have no clear and positive explanation. These movements may have taken place out of a desire for plunder, because of food shortages, pressure of other peoples, or perhaps simply because the Germanic tribes were driven by the characteristic restlessness of all nomadic peoples. In any event, we know that the most important of these Germanic tribes (Goths, Vandals, Burgundians and Alemanni) had apparently reached the Rhine and the Danube basin sometime about 100 B.C. They might well have conquered Gaul (France) had not Roman military power thrust them back to the Rhine frontier where large numbers of them settled permanently. In the fourth and fifth centuries, however, when the imperial frontier collapsed, certain German tribes—Vandals, Visigoths, Franks—penetrated territories lying west of the Rhine. At about the same time the Germanic Angles and Saxons began the conquest of the Roman province of Britain.

What we know of these early Germans comes to us from thin and scattered sources. Only one written work descriptive of them, the *Germania* composed by the Roman historian Tacitus in 98 A.D., has survived. Otherwise we are forced to rely upon bits of surviving folk literature, compilations of Germanic laws, and archeology. On these bases an earlier generation of historians built up an idealized and romanticized picture of these tribesmen as brave, strong, lovers of freedom who gave a distinctive cast to later European legal and political traditions. This is an exaggeration. Nevertheless, some few of their customs did have later influences. Perhaps more importantly, however, though their coming in great numbers contributed to the final breakdown of Roman imperial government, they were made part of Latin Christianity by the process of conversion over a period of time. In this way, they helped to create the later medieval European community of Christendom and thus contributed to the making of Europe.

C.   The Early Division of Christendom and the Byzantine East

Death of the Emperor Justinian (565) ended hopes of reuniting the eastern and western halves of the Roman Empire; the Eastern or Byzantine Empire remained the sole heir to Rome's power. With the passage of time, however, it ceased to be Roman and became almost completely Greek in language and culture.

Loss of Italian possessions to the Lombards, 568-571. Beginning of Islamic conquest of the Eastern Empire, 635-655. Constantinople besieged by Moslems, 673-678 and 717-718. Missionary activities of Saints Cyril and Methodius paved the way for conversion of the Slavic peoples to Orthodox Christianity, 863-865. Prince Vladimir of Russia converted, 989. Final religious schism between Rome and Constantinople, 1054.

Victory of the Seljuk Turks over the Byzantines at Manzikert (1071) marked the beginning of Byzantine decline. Conquest and sack of Constantinople by western Crusaders (Fourth Crusade), 1204. Latin kingdom of Constantinople established, 1204-1261. Reconquest of Constantinople by Emperor Michael VIII, 1261. Rise of the Ottoman Turks in Asia Minor, 1326. Siege and capture of Constantinople by the Ottoman Turks—end of the Eastern Empire, 1453.

The Problem of the Great Schism between East and West: Though theological differences and missionary rivalries were the obvious reasons for the division between the Greek Orthodox and the Latin Churches in 1054, there are certain other things that need to be known about the relations between the two in order to understand their attitudes toward one another over the centuries. While the dispute which led to their division in 1054 was a result of theological disagreement over the use of images in churches, it must also be remembered that the two churches were growing further apart because of cultural and ethnic differences and that the Byzantine Church had to consider political as well as religious divergences among the various peoples who inhabited the eastern empire. In this latter respect, the Eastern Church was never as free as the western Latin Church. It was, after all, a department of the state, in a sense, as the western church was

C. The Early Division of Christendom and the Byzantine East

So long as the Roman empire in the West existed and for some centuries thereafter, the Christian world, though periodically torn by controversy, maintained a nominal unity under the headship of the bishops of Rome (the popes), who, from their central position at the heart of the empire, were able to assert and maintain claims to supremacy over the whole Christian church. With the establishment in the East of a new capital, Constantinople (Byzantium), in the early 4th century, the eastern and western halves of the empire gradually became separate units of ecclesiastical as well as political administration. When the western half of the empire fell, the eastern half continued in existence and insisted, with some justice, that it was the true inheritor of Rome's power. Under the Emperor Justinian (527-565) the Eastern Empire strove to restore Roman unity by conquering the western provinces. When this effort failed, the Eastern Roman empire fell back upon its own resources and took on the cultural characteristics and language of its Greek surroundings. Withal, however, it was profoundly Christian, and its church, the spiritual predecessor of the modern Eastern Orthodox churches, remained in communion with Rome and recognized, at least nominally, the supremacy of the Pope.

In spite of their common Christian heritage, the Byzantine empire and the Roman West were increasingly isolated from one another during the early middle ages. The Eastern Empire was continually involved in a struggle to preserve the old eastern Roman heritage from successive waves of invaders. Though it faced grave difficulties, this Greek empire made skillful use of its military resources and managed to keep its independence and even to make Constantinople the center of a brilliant civilization for nearly a thousand years. Secure in the confidence that the Eastern Empire was the true Rome and its civilization superior to that of the Germanized West (as it was), the Greek church grew increasingly restive at the claims of the Roman popes to speak for the whole Christian church. Theological controversy, further aggravated by missionary rivalry (the Greek church had been successful in carrying its form of Christianity to the Slavic peoples of eastern and northern Europe), finally led to a schism in 1054 which was to divide the Latin and Greek churches thereafter.

Apart from the problem of religion, the existence of the Eastern Empire was of profound importance to the West in other ways. For centuries Constantinople was a bulwark against invaders who might otherwise have made their way deep into the heart of western Europe. At the not and, therefore, could not be so firm about matters of religious orthodoxy as the Latin Church was. This meant that when Rome commanded the Byzantine Church to deal summarily with religious dissenters, the eastern church could not always do so for political reasons. Nevertheless, over the centuries—and, indeed, down to our own time—the two churches have remained very close to one another so far as basic theological assumptions, liturgical forms, and ecclesiastical practices are concerned.

D. The Preservation of Europe : Moslem and Viking

1. The Rise of Islam

A. LIFE OF MOHAMMED, 570-632. Birth at Mecca, 570. Flight (hegira) from Mecca to Medina, 622, altered the character of the new Islamic sect and gave it an opportunity for broader appeal. Compilation of the Koran (the sacred book of Islam), 622-632, revealed its strong ethical bases and its spiritual strength which attracted the Arab tribes. Organization of the commonwealth of Islam at Medina, 622-630. At Mohammed's death, 632, Islam had already displayed the expansionist tendencies that marked its later growth.

B. EXPANSION OF ISLAM, 632-1491. Conquest of Syria, 634-641; Persia, 635-641; Egypt, 639-644; North Africa, 643-711; Spain, 711-715. Invasion of southern France and defeat at Tours by Charles Martel, 732. Breakup of the first great Islamic Empire began, c. 750. Seljuk Turks attacked and took Babylon, 1055. Christian crusaders from the West established the kingdom of Jerusalem, 1099-1187. Christian reconquest of Spain, 1072-1491. Rise of the Ottoman Turks (14th century) led finally to their domination of the Moslem world by the mid-15th century.

C. THE RELIGIOUS TEACHINGS OF ISLAM. The emergence of Islam as a major religion during the early middle ages was of enormous importance in the development of medieval Europe. Not only did many of the writings of the ancient world pass through the hands of Moslem scholars before being transmitted to the Latin West, but Islam by its very existence challenged the religious community of Christendom in a number of stimulating ways.

The important religious fact about Islam from its very

same time, during periods of peace, it was a major exchange point for trade between the West and the Asiatic hinterland.

D. The Preservation of Europe: Moslem and Viking

Though the formation of Europe as we have come to know it in modern times was largely accomplished by the 11th century, this process was continually interrupted and, on occasion, even apparently checked by the threat of outside invasion. The most dangerous of these invaders from the standpoint of future western civilization were the Moslems (Mohammedans) and the Vikings, who struck at the West from opposite ends of Europe.

1. The Rise of Islam

Of the two threats the more dangerous was presented by the followers of Islam (the name which all Moslems give to their religion), for though the Viking raids were disastrous, the Northmen were ultimately Christianized and brought into the community of Europe as the Moslems never were. The latter were followers of the desert prophet Mohammed (570-632), who, in the 7th century, had aroused the zeal of the nomad peoples of Arabia by presenting them with a new religious revelation. Inspired by the new faith to embark upon a series of conquests, the followers of Islam, because of their superior military skills and the high level of their civilization, ultimately menaced the security of early medieval Europe.

Beginning in the 7th century, the Moslems spread rapidly outward from the Arabian peninsula and by the opening of the 8th century had brought under their control large parts of the Near and Middle East, all of North Africa, and Spain. In the West this expansion was finally checked by the Germanic (Frankish) inhabitants of France at the battle of Tours in 732. In the East, however, though the leadership of Islam later passed from the Arabs to the Seljuk Turks and later still to the Ottoman Turks, a relentless, centuries-long pressure against Constantinople finally led to that city's capture in 1453 and the Islamic conquest of large areas in southeastern Europe.

In spite of the inveterate hostility between Christian and Moslem, beginning was its direct and simple appeal to the ethical understanding of the peoples to whom it was preached. Mohammed was not a sophisticated scholar or subtle thinker, and therein lay much of the success of the religion which he founded. The teaching of Islam was unambiguous and easily comprehended. Allah, the Islamic designation for the deity, is a single all-powerful, all-knowing God in the great monotheistic tradition of Judaism and Christianity. Unlike Christianity, however, Islam did not have to develop a complex theology to explain the nature of a divine trinity or why it was that God should have chosen to appear on earth in human form in order to suffer on the cross. Mohammed was not "a partaker of divinity." He was only the last and greatest of the prophets, "the seal of the prophets." Abraham and Christ, according to the view of the Moslem holy book or Koran, were both earlier prophets who simply prepared the way for the coming of Mohammed.

Furthermore, the ethical injunctions laid down in the Koran are stern and demandingly puritanical. The word "Islam" means submission to the will of Allah. Allah rewards those who obey his commands and punishes those who do not. Faithful Moslems are expected to pray regularly and to visit the holy places at Mecca at least once in their lives. They are also expected to avoid drinking and gambling, deal with their fellow men in justice and mercy, practice charity, and adhere to a rigorous code of sexual morality (though the Moslem who can afford it is permitted to have four wives). And, finally, the Moslem is expected to defend the true faith with his very life, if necessary—a requirement which has made Islam one of the most militant of all religions. The really great mass appeal of Islam lay—and still lies—in the essential clarity of its ethical demands. Here there are no doubts as to whether the good man may perish or the evil prosper. The commands of Allah, if obeyed, will give the righteous their due reward without doubt or question.

2. Viking Invasions, 787-1266

First invasion of England by the Danes, 787; continued in force, 856-875. Siege of Paris by Northmen, 886. Founding of the duchy of Normandy by Rollo the Northman, 911. Danish kings ruled England, 1013-1041. Norman conquest it was from the great Islamic centers of learning, particularly in Spain, that much knowledge of ancient civilization, lost to the West since Rome's fall, came to light in medieval Europe. Moslem scholars translated and preserved the works of Aristotle which were later introduced into 13th-century Europe with enormous intellectual impact. Moreover, the techniques and skills of Arab traders, the mathematics of Arab savants, and the scientific devices of Arab technology also contributed much to the medieval West.

2. Viking Invasions

The causes of the great Viking invasions of Europe are still something of a mystery. A desire for loot and plunder is not alone sufficient to explain why these bands of freebooters irrupted into Europe with such force and frequency during the early middle ages. Their raids came in waves of varying intensity and were frequently separated by long periods of quiescence. Apparently a combination of causes—hope of gain, the political disunity of ancient Scandinavia, and population pressures in their homelands—drove them forth to plunder the coasts of Europe for more than 400 years. Once they had been converted to Christianity, however, they rapidly assimilated to the customs and traditions of western Christendom. Rapacious in their desire for plunder and irrational in the heat of battle, they, nonetheless, were a people of intelligence as well as energy who ruled the lands they conquered with astuteness and skill. By the 11th century they had established a group of feudal states whose stability and administrative efficiency made them unique in medieval Europe. In northern France they founded the duchy of Normandy, whose power rivaled that of French kings, and, in Italy, the kingdom of Sicily. Their greatest success, however, came with the Norman conquest of England in 1066, as a result of which they were able to create the strongest and most highly centralized of feudal monarchies. In the 12th and 13th centuries their remote colony of Iceland on the farthest edge of the medieval world was to develop a native literature unequaled for its vigor and brilliance anywhere in Europe.

of southern Italy, 1042-1068. Invasion and conquest of England by William of Normandy (battle of Hastings), 1066. Normans conquered Sicily, 1072-1091, and established kingdom of Sicily, 1091-1266.

E.   Reconsolidation of the West: Revival of the Imperial Idea

1.   Charlemagne's Empire, 768-814

Accession of Charlemagne to Frankish throne, 768. Defeated Lombards in Italy and assumed title of king, 773-774. Conquered the Saxons, 785; Bavarians, 787-788; and Avars, 795-796. Pope Leo III crowned Charlemagne Emperor of the West at Rome, 800. Death of Charlemagne, 814.

2.   Successors of Charlemagne, 814-987

Reign of Louis the Pious, 814-840. Treaty of Verdun, 843, divided empire among three heirs and thus separated the historical areas of modern France and Germany. Henry the Fowler became king of Germany, 919-936. Otto the Great of Germany crowned emperor at Rome, 962; beginning of the Germanization of the Holy Roman Empire. Hugh Capet crowned king of France, 987.

3.   The Carolingian Renaissance

Charlemagne re-established the palace school for the improvement of ecclesiastical learning under the direction of Alcuin of York, 782-796. Also founded libraries for the preservation of Latin manuscripts and restored classical learning through the promotion of scholarship. The important thing about Carolingian society, however, apart from its purely intellectual achievements, was that Charlemagne tried to apply intelligence and rationalized practices to the affairs of government. Unfortunately, neither the resources nor the number of educated persons were sufficient to guarantee the permanence of Carolingian administrative effectiveness.

E.   Reconsolidation of the West: Revival of the Imperial Idea

By the end of the 8th century at least one of the Germanic successor states, the kingdom of the Franks (which comprised almost all of modern France and part of modern Germany), seemed capable of restoring the lost unity of the Western Empire. The hope of such a restoration had been kept alive by the papacy, and that hope seemed to become a reality with the rise to power of the strong Frankish king, Charlemagne (768-814). Under him the kingdom of the Franks had become a great military power with a remarkably efficient feudal government. Unfortunately for papal desires, these characteristics alone were not sufficient to make Charlemagne's realm into a new Roman Empire. No feudal society could successfully reproduce the centralized bureaucracy or maintain the permanent tax-supported military organization of the earlier empire. Without these, reviving Rome's universal dominion was impossible. Nonetheless, the effort was made by Pope Leo III who, on Christmas day in the year 800, crowned Charlemagne Emperor of the West. In the end, this coronation proved to be only a futile gesture, for, despite his great unifying achievement and his success in reintroducing the lost cultural traditions of antiquity to the north European peoples (Carolingian Renaissance), Charlemagne's empire scarcely outlasted his own lifetime. After his death it was divided among his descendants, and the division was confirmed permanently by the Treaty of Verdun in 843.

Undeterred by this initial failure, later popes attempted, once again, to revive the empire and, in the 10th century, helped to create the Holy Roman Empire by crowning the German prince Otto the Great as emperor. By that time, however, it was already too late. The various feudal kingdoms of the West were too strong and too firmly entrenched to surrender their sovereignty to any imperial overlord, even one backed by the authority of the papacy.

EVENTS AND DEFINITIONS

A. The Medieval Papacy and the Idea of Universality

Foundation of the monastery of Cluny, 910; spread of its influence, 910-950. The monk Hildebrand (later Pope Gregory VII) led the reform movement in the church, 1054-1085. As pope he forced the Emperor Henry IV to submit to papal authority by a public act of penance at Canossa, 1077.

Nature and significance of the Gregorian Reform Movement: The Gregorian reform movement was not simply an

CHAPTER 6

The High Middle Ages

THE ESSENTIAL MOVEMENT

The period of the high middle ages (12th through 14th centuries) saw the culmination of what is now recognized as a great civilization. In those three centuries many isolated and scattered strands of historical development came together to form a complex cultural unity which, while it accepted the goals and aspirations of Christian belief, was, nonetheless, freer in expression and more diverse in its interests than former historians were wont to think. This civilization contributed far more to the development of some of the later institutions and traditions of the modern world than was previously thought. Far from having been a time of repression and stagnation, this era of history was rather a period of great achievement and originality.

A. The Medieval Papacy and the Idea of Universality

The high middle ages marked the peak of papal power and authority. The reasons for this development, which culminated in the pontificate of Innocent III (1198-1216), are to be found in a number of revolutionary changes that made the medieval church into an effective international administrative system run by an intellectual elite of men whose training and abilities were far higher than those of the rest of society. Through the patient work of these persons over many generations, the church was largely freed of its dependence upon nobles and kings, and the papal extension of the earlier Cluniac reform movement mentioned in Section A (Essential Movement). It was in many ways a totally new movement which came into being as the original reforming impulses of the older Clunias movement died away. Its three other great leaders (apart from Pope Gregory VII, 1073-1085, or Hildebrand) were Paschal II (1099-1118) and two cardinals, Peter Damiani (d. 1072) and Humbert of Silva Candida (d. 1061). These four men were not only responsible for the rejuvenation of the life of the church and the exaltation of papal authority but stimulated an intense piety that reached out to every corner of Christendom. This new piety made it possible for the papacy of the 12th and 13th centuries to direct and guide the affairs of medieval Europe as no other single institution has ever done in history. Men came to believe in the truth of Christian revelation and the Church's teachings as never before or since. Some scholars have even argued that this change was so radical as to constitute a great revolution in men's ways of thought and action. Though this conclusion has been questioned by other historians, it is true that the church's authority did depend upon the important fact that large numbers of human beings were willing to accept its teachings unquestioningly. Furthermore, this new and intense piety prepared the way for the founding of the two greatest of medieval mendicant (begging) monastic orders: the Franciscans founded by St. Francis of Assisi (1182-1226) and the Dominicans founded by Saint Dominic (1170-1221). From the latter order came Thomas Aquinas (1225-1274), the greatest of medieval scholastic philosophers.

Proclamation of the first crusade by Pope Urban II, 1095.

Compromise over lay investiture in England and France, 1107. Concordat of Worms, 1122, settled differences between pope and Holy Roman Emperor over lay investiture in German lands.

Innocent III (1198-1216) asserted the supremacy of the papacy over all Christendom: forced John of England to acknowledge the pope as feudal overlord, 1213; suppressed Albigensian heresy in the south of France by formal crusade, 1208-1213. Under Pope Innocent the medieval church reached its highest peak of administrative effectiveness. Innocent's reforms and changes were summed up in the decrees of the office was made the focus of an administrative authority that reached into every corner of Latin Christendom.

The revolution which made this possible began with the founding, in the 10th century, of the Cluniac order of monks (named for the abbey of Cluny in southern France). By stressing the importance of monastic discipline in their personal lives and of canon (church) law in the conduct of ecclesiastical business, the monks of Cluny were able to initiate a vast reform movement in the church during the 10th and 11th centuries. As a result, many serious ecclesiastical abuses were corrected and, more importantly, the right to choose the popes passed into the control of an elective body (the college of cardinals) and out of the hands of the Holy Roman Emperors who had previously nominated the pontiffs. Once the churchmen had freed their own highest office of lay control, they pushed other reforms with such vigor that the quality of the clergy steadily improved and the standards of religious teaching rose throughout medieval Europe. The victory was not easily won, however. The Holy Roman Emperors and most other secular rulers were opposed to an independent clergy who might challenge their own authority. Furthermore, they were anxious to retain the right of nomination to high ecclesiastical office within their own territories, since by reason of their offices the archbishops, bishops, and abbots were usually also feudal landholders or state officials with so much secular authority that no king could safely allow the church to have the sole power of choosing them. While the papacy gained its own independence, therefore, it had to struggle throughout the middle ages for the right to nominate other high ecclesiastical officeholders. In this conflict over lay investiture the church's weapons were excommunication (the power to deny an individual the sacraments, i.e., baptism, communion, confirmation, etc.), and interdict (the power to cut off an entire country from the ministrations of religion in order to force its rulers to submit). These potent weapons were sufficient, in an age when men accepted the church's spiritual authority without question, to make the popes nominal overlords of all Christendom. The assumption that justified this great authority was based upon an ancient claim long accepted by the supporters of papal supremacy but seldom put into practice before the 11th century. This was the claim that the popes, as a consequence of the power originally conferred by Christ upon St. Peter, the first pontiff, were responsible as Christ's vicars for the spiritual welfare of all mankind, while secular rulers were responsible only for the welfare of their own subjects—and only in this world. As a natural conclusion of this theory, it was believed by papal supporters that the power of the popes was universal and thus transcended the authority of temporal monarchs.

Fourth Lateran Council (1215). It was this council that first clearly defined the seven sacraments as baptism, holy eucharist, confession (penance), confirmation, marriage, ordination, and extreme unction. Boniface VIII (1294-1303) became the last of the all-powerful popes as the "Babylonian captivity" (1305-1376) saw the papacy transferred to Avignon in the south of France where popes fell under the influence of French kings.

The Great Schism (1378-1417) marked the division of the church between two rival popes. John Wyclif initiated the Lollard movement in England by challenging the church's theology, 1380. Wyclifite influence gave rise to the Hussite heresy (named for John Hus) in Bohemia, *c.*1400. Council of Constance ended the Great Schism and restored the unity of the Papacy, 1414-1418.

B.   The Rise of the Feudal Monarchies

1.   England, 1066-1485

Conquest of England by William Duke of Normandy in 1066 introduced the continental system of feudalism and established a tradition of strong and effective kingship. Beginning with William the Conqueror (1066-1087) and continuing through the reigns of three strong kings—Henry I (1100-1135), Henry II (1154-1189), and Edward I (1272-1307)—England developed the most effectively centralized feudal state in Europe. At the same time English kings embarked upon a policy of expansion that saw a large part of the British Isles brought under their rule and made them at various times until the middle of the 15th century masters of great territorial holdings in France.

A. DEVELOPMENT OF THE ENGLISH STATE. Domesday Book (1086) surveyed the whole of England and gave to English kings a body of statistical information not available to other feudal monarchs. Organization of the exchequer in the reign of Henry I (1100-1135) facilitated the relatively efficient collection of the king's revenues. Permanent court of professional judges organized (1178), out of which evolved the later courts of common law (king's bench, exchequer, and common pleas). English barons forced John (1199-1216) to sign the Great

The pope, then, was accountable for the "cure of souls"; and, since this responsibility was a far greater one than that of any king, conflicts between the spiritual and temporal powers had to be resolved in favor of the former. On the basis of this claim, Pope Innocent III, in the 13th century, was able to assert not only a spiritual but a feudal lordship over all the Latin West.

B. The Rise of Feudal Monarchies

Despite the papacy's great success, medieval kings contrived to hold their own in the struggle and even to expand their powers. To do so they had to accomplish two things: first, they had to destroy the localized authority of great feudal nobles whose power often threatened their own; and, second, they had to create a centralized government bureaucracy which would enable them to rule without having to depend upon the churchmen or the great feudal lords for the carrying on of the routine business of state. They moved toward these goals not with any carefully thought-out long-range plan but by day-to-day effort. Sometimes the royal power was checked and the process of expansion even reversed, but over the centuries it grew steadily until the highly centralized, absolute monarchies of the early modern period had come into being.

During all this time European kings had to perform a skillful political juggling act. On the one hand, they had to make use of the church and churchmen to strengthen royal government and weaken the feudal nobility. To do so they borrowed from the church the administrative techniques and experience which only the church possessed. On the other hand, they had to be careful not to make the church itself so strong that it would become, in the end, as dangerous to their authority as the feudal nobles. This problem was further intensified by the difficulty of financing the kind of government they sought through the methods available in a feudal society. Royal revenues did not take the form of regularly stipulated payments from all their subjects for the support of the state but of feudal

Charter (Magna Carta), 1215, and thus to recognize the validity of the feudal contract; limited the power of the king. Simon de Montfort, head of a faction of rebellious barons, summoned a parliament, 1265. Edward I called first "model" parliament, in 1295. Parliament developed and became a permanent English institution during the 14th and 15th centuries. Social unrest of the Hundred Years' War led to Peasants' Revolt, 1381. Period of anarchy in the mid-14th century culminated in Wars of the Roses, civil strife between two rival factions for control of the English throne, 1455-1485. Henry VII defeated Richard III at battle of Bosworth (1485) to end civil wars and restore order.

   B. EXPANSION OF ENGLAND, 1066-1485. First English invasion of Ireland, 1169. Loss of the duchy of Normandy to France, 1204. Conquest of Wales, 1276-1284. Edward I attempted to conquer Scotland, 1292-1307; Scots defeated his son, Edward II, at Bannockburn, 1314. Independence of Scotland recognized at Treaty of Northampton, 1328. Outbreak of the Hundred Years' War (1337-1453) between England and France saw England at first victorious under Edward III (1327-1377) and later under Henry V (1413-1422); England finally forced to relinquish all its French possessions but Calais.

2.   France, 987-1483

   The great problems of the medieval French monarchy were to curb the power of a strong feudal nobility and, in the later middle ages, to win back lands that had been lost to England and the dukes of Burgundy. The first problem was doubly difficult for the French kings, because they had not conquered France as William the Conqueror had England, but were in fact only the greatest of feudal landholders—and sometimes not even that. What they had to do gradually over many generations was conquer their own nobles and make them obey royal law. Under a series of strong kings, whose good fortune it was to remain unbroken in the male line between 987 and 1328, the French monarchy steadily extended its power outward from the environs of Paris by marriage and conquest. The most important of these kings were Hugh Capet (the founder of the Capetian line), 987-996; Philip II (Augustus), 1180-1223, who won back the duchy of Normandy dues or aids which were granted the king by his vassals on some extraordinary occasion when the king's own income was insufficient. The regular income that went to pay for the king's personal needs and to support the developing bureaucracy of the royal household had to come from the rents on his own personal estates (demesne lands). From the 12th century onward one of the major tasks of the feudal monarch was thus to preserve and increase his personal lands and, since the revenues from these were not sufficient to meet all his needs, to convert the irregular feudal dues into a regular form of revenue. In attempting to do these things, however, medieval kings further strained their relations with the church on one side and the feudal nobles on the other.

The conflict with the church was intensified because the 13th century had seen the consummation of that internal administrative revolution in ecclesiastical government begun about 300 years before. The great autonomous, international bureaucracy of the church had need not only of great financial resources but also of intellectually trained manpower. Since both were limited and both were demanded by church and state alike, the competition between popes and kings for these inadequate resources was intense. Both simultaneously brought pressures to bear on feudal society and each, in so doing, sought to limit the other's right to make use of lands and revenues. In the desperate search for new revenues, medieval kings fell back upon a device which, in time, would lead to even greater conflicts between themselves and their subjects. It was during this period that feudal representative assemblies—the English parliament, French estates general, German diet—came into existence. Though the concept of representative government had long been known in the church and had been carried over into secular government in many localized areas of Europe, medieval monarchs in the 13th and 14th centuries began to make greater use of it to serve their own financial and administrative needs. Monarchs found it to their advantage to consult with the representatives of all the important feudal classes or estates in order to. secure their co-operation in getting money for the royal treasury. The latter, in their turn, found that the representative assemblies served as a means of limiting royal authority and protecting their own interests. Thus, in many parts of Europe, these representative bodies came to be serious deterrents to royal power, and the issue of sovereignty raised by this new conflict had to be settled at a later date, sometimes in favor of the crown (as in France) and sometimes (as in England) in favor of the representative assembly.

Through all the vicissitudes of conflict with the church and the feudal aristocracy, monarchical power continued to expand in many parts of from England in 1204; Louis IX (St. Louis, the crusading king), 1226-1270; and Philip IV (the Fair), 1285-1314.

A. THE HUNDRED YEARS' WAR, 1337-1453. The Hundred Years' War, which turned out to be a long and disastrous interlude in the history of both France and England, began with English successes at Crécy (1346) and Poitiers (1356) that led to the conquest of extensive French territories. The war started for three causes: (1) the ambitions of Edward III of England (1327-1377); (2) the want of a male heir to the French monarchy at the death of the last Capetian king in 1328, which opened the door to claims by Edward III, whose mother was a French princess, and (3) a longstanding conflict between the French and English crowns over the administration of feudal lands held by English kings in France. After a period of abeyance, Henry V of England (1413-1422) renewed the conflict at the battle of Agincourt (1415) and forced the French to recognize his rights to the French throne, which he further confirmed by marrying the daughter of the king of France. After Henry's death the French monarchy under Charles VII (1422-1461), with whose name is associated the French heroine Joan of Arc, gradually began the recovery of lost lands and the expulsion of the English, goals which were not finally achieved until 1453.

B. RESULTS OF THE HUNDRED YEARS' WAR. For France the results were disastrous: the country was ravaged, property destroyed, large numbers of lives lost. For England, though the war was not fought on English soil, the results were also bad; the English monarchy was weakened, society was torn by dissension, and the state was bankrupted. The most important over-all effect was that nationalism in its modern form seems to have had its beginnings in the intense rivalries between the two nations. Under Louis XI (1461-1483) France began to recover and finally eliminated the menace of the duchy of Burgundy, which had consistently allied itself with England during most of the struggle. By Louis's death in 1483 France had emerged as a reunified nation with one of the strongest monarchies in Europe.

3. The Holy Roman Empire.

The history of the Holy Roman Empire during the middle ages is a story of missed opportunities. Originally intended

Europe. The most notable exception was the Holy Roman Empire, whose rulers, after a long struggle with the great feudal lords, finally sank to a position where their title was all but empty. In England and France, however, the story was very different. As a result of the Norman Conquest in 1066, English monarchs were able to reorganize the state and to make the feudal lords into tractable servants. In France this development was somewhat slower but by the end of the 13th century there, too, the monarch and the royal government had triumphed. An important reason for these successes is to be found in the popularity of the monarchy. Medieval kings, by creating a central administration which dispensed justice far less partially than did the courts of the petty feudal lordlings and by giving to feudal society a stability which it had previously lacked, made themselves and their governments popular with lesser men—small landholders, merchants, artisans—who had suffered from the lawlessness and caprice of feudal disorder. Above the whole of society, the king gradually came to be the symbol of an impersonal, impartial, effective state power, which, whatever its shortcomings, represented the idea of justice and the rule of law.

as the medieval successor to the universal empire of Rome, it promised at one point in the 10th and 11th centuries to become the strongest state in Europe. The long struggle with the papacy, however, and the inability of the medieval emperors to consolidate permanently the bases of their political authority kept the Holy Roman Empire from achieving its fullest potentialities. Although the emperors tried to extend their sway over other regions (most notably Italy) the medieval Empire remained essentially a Germanic institution. The most important events in its medieval history were as follows: Otto I (936-973), first true Holy Roman Emperor, crowned at Rome, 962. Empire reached its peak of greatness under Henry III (1039-1056). Henry IV (1056-1106) humbled as a result of investiture controversy by Gregory VII at Canossa, 1077. German penetration of Slavic lands east of Elbe river ("Drang nach Osten") begun, c. 1130; continued by Teutonic Knights, c. 1190-1400. Golden Bull (1356) gave seven permanent electors right to choose the emperor. Election of Albert II (1438-1439), first of the Hapsburg dynasty which ruled the Empire until its demise (1806).

C. Economic Growth and the Expansion of Medieval Europe, c. 1000-1500

1 Growth of Urban Life

Movement for independent control of their affairs began among the towns of Italy, 11th century. Institution of the Grand Council of Venice, 1063. Lombard League of towns defeated Emperor Frederick I (battle of Legnano), 1176.

Movement spread northward as feudal monarchs granted free charters to towns: London given charter by Henry I, 1131. Formation of the north German Hanseatic League, 13th century. By 1500 a city like London probably had a population in the neighborhood of 80,000.

The pace of economic and technological change. An earlier generation of historians was wont to believe that the great changes in the techniques of European production that led to increased European wealth occurred during the course of what was sometimes called the Commercial Revolution of the 16th and 17th centuries. This period, they believed, was actually

C. Economic Growth and the Expansion of Medieval Europe

One of the significant and obvious developments of the modern world is that movement, usually described as "the expansion of Europe," which has seen the spread of European peoples and their civilization to every quarter of the globe. For long, historians customarily thought of this expansion as beginning in the Age of Discovery from the 15th century onward. Conversely, they thought of the medieval period as a time of economic and social stagnation in which Europe was a self-contained economic unit incapable of expansion outside its own geographical limits. Just as we have been forced to revise our opinion about the middle ages in other matters, so, too, have we been forced to revise our opinion in this. Greater knowledge has made it plain that the Europe of the high middle ages was a hive of economic and technological activity wherein was taking place a great deal of internal expansion which extended the local frontiers of European civilization and laid the groundwork without which the overseas expansion of a later period would have been impossible.

the time when the system commonly called capitalism, i.e., commercial and industrial production for profit, actually came into being. More recently, however, with the expansion of our knowledge of medieval economic and social history, this view has been drastically revised. It is now believed that the beginnings of European productive expansion actually occurred during the course of the 10th and 11th centuries (c. 950-1100). This was not only the period which saw a rapid expansion of towns and cities but it also marked the beginnings of that process of capital accumulation which was to continue intermittently throughout the history of Europe and the western world. Down to that time the Byzantine and Arab worlds were far ahead of Latin Europe in economic development. This lead the Byzantines and Arabs continued to maintain throughout the middle ages, but the gap was gradually narrowed as generations passed until about 1500 when the West assumed that clear economic and technological lead which it has never relinquished.

So far as we can now determine, this transformation was made possible by a "commercial revolution" in 11th-century Italy which came about because the Italians had improved production to a point where they had a surplus of commodities to sell to other Mediterranean regions. From Italy this commercial expansion spread across Europe and was paralleled by the development of a "northern trade" which encompassed north Germany, the Low Countries, northern France, and England. Improvements in business techniques (in which Italy long led the rest of Europe) and technological innovations (improvements in the use of horsepower, introduction of windmills, and increased use of waterpower) had much to do with it. Equally, if not more important, however, were changes in society itself—the development of relatively strong feudal states, the decline of violence, a rise in literacy, and the attempt to apply rationality to human affairs. All of these created a general sense of social stability and optimism which are needed for expanding societies. This period of expansion lasted down into the 14th century when a period of economic social stagnation appears to have set in from which Europe did not begin to recover until toward the end of the 15th century.

1. Growth of Urban Life

One of the more significant aspects of this development is to be seen in the growth of European towns and cities from the 10th century onward. Historians dispute the reasons for this urban growth but none deny its far-reaching consequences. Economically, the rise of cities had two important long-range effects. It raised the standard of living and the economic power of important segments of the European population and thus made possible the accumulation of large amounts of fluid capital which, by a process of continual reinvestment, ultimately made the European economic system the most dynamic the world has ever seen. Furthermore, the stimulus of intercity trade not only brought Europeans into closer contact with one another but also, as in the urban revolution of the ancient world, helped to disseminate ideas and techniques more widely than ever before. Business skills and manufacturing processes, though crude by modern standards, were extensively developed. Money came to be used widely as a medium of exchange. With these innovations, the whole of western Europe began the long process of transformation from a predominantly agricultural to a predominantly urban civilization.

In the wake of this transformation came social and political changes of great consequence. The increase in communications among the great urban centers in all parts of Europe helped to break down the localism of medieval life and in those areas where feudal kings were strong actually fostered the increase of central power. To accommodate the new cities the social relations of feudal society had to be drastically modified. Merchants and traders needed a freedom of movement which forced a relaxation of the bonds of feudal obligation. With greater freedom the merchant became a figure of more consequence in European life. His wealth, energy, and intelligence gave him a greater political significance with the result that his interests were more carefully considered by the state. Nor was the merchant class the only group affected by this transformation. The increasing needs of large centers of population required greater agricultural production so that farming was no longer pursued solely for the cultivators' subsistence but was undertaken to produce salable surpluses for city markets. Since these surpluses were usually paid for with money, many serfs and smallholders were able to buy themselves free of customary services to their feudal overlords. As this process went on, the old system of feudal-manorial relations gradually gave way to a system of greater economic and social freedom. By the 16th century the institution of serfdom was rapidly disappearing throughout western Europe.

2.   Rural Life, Colonization, and Conquest

A. IMPROVEMENT IN AGRICULTURAL TECHNIQUES. Development of more effective harness made possible increased utilization of horses in plowing. Mouldboard plow effectively improved preparation for crop planting. Both added significantly to medieval agricultural productivity, 12th century. Opening up of fertile lands to which were applied new techniques in rotation and fertilization. Growth of farming surpluses and specialization of production, e.g. English wool.

B. COLONIZATION. Continuous settlement of European border or "march" lands from the 11th century onward. German colonists conquered the Slavs beyond the Elbe River and introduced west European agricultural techniques into the area. Settlement and partial conquest of Celtic fringe areas: English invasion and settlement of Ireland (11th century), conquest of Wales (13th century), and attempt to conquer Scotland (14th century).

C. CRUSADING MOVEMENTS, 11TH-15TH CENTURIES. ■ (1) In the Middle East, First crusade (1099-1101) captured Jerusalem and established western feudal state in Palestine (kingdom of Jerusalem). Saladin recaptured Jerusalem (battle of Hattin), 1187. Third crusade recaptured Acre from the Moslems, 1191. Fourth crusade captured and sacked Constantinople, 1204. Fifth and last major crusade captured and held Damietta (North Africa) for two years, 1219-1221. From that time forward no major effort was made to recover the Holy Land, and the West remained on the defensive against the Turks. ■ (2) In Europe. The Order of Teutonic Knights, originally organized in the Holy Land, was invited to Prussia, 1229, to crusade against the pagan Slavs; it became a powerful social and cultural force in the Baltic region during the 13th and 14th centuries. Reconquest of Spain: Defeat of the Moslems at Las Navas de Tolosa (1212) began the major phase of Christian reconquest. Ferdinand III of Castile captured Cordova (1236) and Seville (1248). Fall of Granada (1491) saw the end of the last Moslem state in Spain.

2.   Rural Life, Colonization, and Conquest

As we have seen, the most important change in European rural life resulted from the growth of cities. There were other changes, however, particularly in agricultural technique and estate management, which also helped to change the social structure and to increase the wealth of Europe. As early as the 12th century some countries were already producing specialized agricultural commodities (English wool, which was the focus of a specialized trade, first with Italy and then with Flanders, is one example) which enabled them to concentrate their skills in order to increase output. The result, though our evidence is scanty, was a rise in population and an increase in demand for land and commodities of all kinds. Largely as a result of this pressure, undeveloped lands were opened up in various parts of Europe, particularly along the borderlands in territories occupied by peoples like the Slavs and Celts. Elsewhere, these expansionist tendencies were reinforced by religious zeal, though it should be made plain that in many cases the religious motive was as strong or stronger than economic desire. In Spain the Moslems were pushed steadily back until by the 14th century their former great holdings had all but disappeared. At the opposite end of the Mediterranean the story was somewhat different. There a series of crusades, first launched in 1095 at papal instigation, had created the shortlived feudal kingdom of Jerusalem. Nor was this crusading effort always directed against Moslems. In the 13th century Christian crusaders captured and plundered Constantinople, which for a time became a Latinized state. These eastern conquests were never permanent, however, and by the second half of the 13th century only a few scattered outposts in the eastern Mediterranean remained in western hands.

D. Medieval Culture

1. Medieval Philosophy

Medieval philosophy has often been looked upon as a kind of sterile and meaningless intellectual exercise in which men only sought to prove the truth of a Christian revelation which they already accepted as a matter of faith. In one sense this judgment is true, but it fails in understanding that the philosophical accomplishments of medieval thinkers were still highly significant for all of that. The development of a rationalized Christian theology, as we noticed earlier (see p. 59), is, after all, one of the unique facts about Christianity which distinguishes it from most other great world religions. What made the role of medieval thinkers significant in its development is that certain of them, most notably Abelard and Thomas Aquinas (for both see below), strove mightily to apply to it the processes of human reason *because* they had no wish to accept it solely on the basis of faith. Had they not undertaken to explain Christian belief in rational human terms, Christianity and indeed the whole western intellectual tradition might never have evolved along lines later taken by both. The long debate, for example, over the problem of universals well illustrates the nature of their intellectual striving. In the argument as to whether the general concepts in our minds such as truth, justice, beauty, God, church, state, etc., have real existence outside our minds they were simply re-examining one of the most persistent questions of western philosophy which is with us even today. One school of thought approved by the church and known as "realists" believed that such concepts did have a "real" existence. Their opponents, known as "nominalists," believed that all general ideas (mankind, for example) have reality only because we know about particulars (individual men). They did not solve the problem but by their very discussion of it they helped to make close rational inquiry concerning the process of knowing an important part of the western tradition.

St. Anselm of Bec and Canterbury (1034?-1109) offered his "one sentence" proof of the existence of God arrived at by logical method.

Abelard (1079-1142) in his *Sic et Non (Yes or No?)* applied reason to the writings of the church fathers in order

D. Medieval Culture

As it was with medieval economic expansion, so it was also with medieval culture. Despite the pervasive authority of the church and its system of theology which provided answers, in broad outline, to all the Big Questions about man and his place in the universe, the intellectual activity of medieval men was neither so arid nor futile as it has sometimes seemed. It is true that the middle ages did not reach a high level of scientific achievement and that there were real limitations to human speculation. But, in spite of these, medieval thinkers made notable contributions to human knowledge in an atmosphere of freedom no more restricted than that of some 20th-century societies.

1. Medieval Philosophy

In the field of philosophy the greatest accomplishment of the middle ages was its completion of the process by which the learning of antiquity was finally incorporated into Christian thought. This work of incorporation had been going forward since the days of the early church fathers, but in the 13th century it was to be culminated with the absorption by the Christian West of the whole body of Aristotle's writings. The accomplishment was by no means easy, for there had been continuous resistance over the centuries to every attempt on the part of Christian scholars to make use of what were called "profane" writings. The truth of Christianity, it was asserted by enemies of secular learning, had been revealed in scripture and the traditions of the church. Since these were all-sufficient for human salvation, there was little need to delve into studies that were irrelevant to the great task of preparing men for a life immortal. If medieval philosophers had really been so completely lacking in intellectual curiosity or so restricted in their outlook as is sometimes said, they would have been content to accept this judgment and let the matter rest. But they were not, and therein lay the greatness of their achievement.

By the late 12th century an intellectual crisis was reached when the works of Aristotle, translated from Arab sources, began to make their way into western Europe. Within a few decades of their appearance heretical opinions, evidently stimulated by the new ideas, began to be expressed in many centers of learning, particularly at the University of Paris; and church authorities moved quickly to suppress the dangerous Aristotelian writings. But two great scholar-philosophers now came forward to undertake the difficult task of assimilating Aristotle without, at the same time, creating heresies. Albertus Magnus (d. 1280) and Thomas Aquinas (1225-1274) between them accomplished the collection and into prove the truth of the Christian faith; his effort was condemned by the church.

Gradual recovery of the works of Aristotle (Aristotelian *corpus*), particularly after the reconquest of Toledo (Spain) in 1085, led to attempts to incorporate his writings into Christian thought.

Albertus Magnus (St. Albert the Great), 1206-1280, collected and commented upon Aristotle's works.

St. Thomas Aquinas, 1225-1274, incorporated Aristotelian knowledge into Christian theology *(Summa Theologica).*

2.   Rise of the Universities

Since many of the universities evolved out of earlier monastic or cathedral schools, it is difficult to say just when the first of them came into existence. Many of them began as scholastic guilds, that is, spontaneous unions of teachers and students. Among the earlier and more famous of the university foundations were Salerno in Italy, 10th-11th centuries; Bologna, 11th century; Paris (the most famous of the medieval universities), 1150-1170; Oxford, late 12th century; and Cambridge, early 13th century.

3.   Medieval Literature and Art

A. LITERATURE. Heroic epic *(Beowulf* and the *Nibelungenlied)* constituted the major literary form before 1100; largely folk inspired. ■ About the 11th century three new forms appeared: (1) the *chansons de geste,* like the *Song of Roland,* which were tales of heroic deeds; (2) the poetry of the troubadours, which dealt with chivalry, courtesy, and courtly love; and (3) the great poetic legends like the Arthurian and Grail legends which reflected strong Christian influences. In the later middle ages, particularly in the 14th century, poems of social criticism appeared. Among the best known of these was William Langland's *Vision of Piers Plowman.* Better known, though it is something more than a work of social criticism, is Geoffrey Chaucer's (1340-1400) *Canterbury Tales.* The most popular medieval poem, however, was *The Romance of the Rose,* the first part of which was written by William de Lorris (13th century). The work was a long ingenious love poem that combined pagan alledexing of Aristotle's thought and its recasting in Christian terms. When the work of Aquinas *(Summa Theologica)* was completed, it was immediately accepted by the church and became a central part of medieval Christian theology. Later this adoption of Aristotle was to have a stultifying effect on the development of scientific and other thought, because Aristotelian learning came to be accepted too slavishly. In the ultimate, however, the preservation of Greek philosophy within the Christian tradition was to help the intellectual development of the West even more than it hindered, for the Aristotelian system assumed the existence of an ordered universe explainable in rational terms. This assumption, when linked with empirical method, helped forge the intellectual tools of modern science.

2. The Rise of the Universities

Perhaps the most original contribution of the medieval world to modern cultural development was the specialized center of advanced studies known as the university. Schools of philosophy had existed in ancient Athens, and something like them had been revived in the days of Charlemagne. Throughout the early middle ages, however, monasteries and abbeys had undertaken to impart a knowledge of advanced subjects if there happened to be a distinguished scholar or group of scholars attached to a particular monastic center. In the 12th century, probably as results of the growing need for men with intellectual training for the administrative posts of the church and of the rise in intellectual standards following the ecclesiastical reforms of the 10th and 11th centuries, there grew up a number of schools attached to great cathedrals. These tended to attract students from all over Europe and in time were organized into university corporations. The course of studies followed a formalized pattern leading ultimately to degrees in the liberal arts, theology, law, or medicine. During the 13th century the University of Paris was the most famous of these new centers of learning and set the model for other university foundations—including Oxford and Cambridge—throughout the north of Europe. The vigor of late medieval intellectual life may best be seen in the fact that by the end of the middle ages some 80 universities had come into existence in all parts of Europe, from Cracow in the East to Lisbon in the West and from Upsala in Sweden to Catania in Sicily.

3. Medieval Literature and Art

Medieval literature, despite the otherworldliness of the age and the influence of religious themes, was still extremely varied. Great epic poems gory with Christian ideals. The greatest of medieval poems, *The Divine Comedy* of Dante Alighieri (1265-1321), is a wonderful combination of art and reason. Dante summarized the thought of his own time within a literary framework of great beauty, a combination achieved by only a few great writers.

B. MEDIEVAL ART. Medieval architecture, more than any other art form, reflected the dominant religious tone of the age. Gothic cathedrals were co-operative enterprises that required the work of many hands for generations. The Gothic style, which originated in northern France during the 12th century, was characterized by (1) the pointed arch and vault, which made it possible to rest the ceiling and roof upon a relatively small number of slender columns and buttresses rather than upon massive continuous walls; (2) the space in the resultant skeleton wall could be filled with broad expanses of stained glass; (3) the result was that the Gothic church interior was always filled with light of various hues; and (4) the stone surfaces, wherever men could reach, were covered with traceries and carvings.

like the Anglo-Saxon *Beowulf* and the French *Song of Roland*, as well as the chivalric poetry of the troubadours and the *Arthurian Legend*, attest to the vitality of medieval literary expression. Perhaps its greatest single production is to be found in that massive combination of art and intellect, *The Divine Comedy* of Dante (1265-1321), which represents one of the most successful efforts ever made to combine the whole body of thought of a particular period with a narrative of surpassing artistry. The other great contribution of medieval men in the sphere of the arts was Gothic architecture. Originating in northern France, it reached its peak in the 12th and 13th centuries with great cathedrals whose stone tracery and stained-glass windows combined to give unity to an art form which was intended to be a perfect manifestation of esthetics and religious faith.

CHAPTER 7

Renaissance and Reformation

THE ESSENTIAL MOVEMENT

The terms "Renaissance" and "Reformation" have been used for so long to describe certain definite periods of European history that it is difficult to think of any others to take their places. Yet, to some extent, both are misnomers.

The word "Renaissance" means rebirth and implies that the history of the middle ages was of little relative importance, socially or culturally. Since we know that the medieval period was far more productive and original than was once believed, the period of the Renaissance (14th through 16th centuries) has now come to be thought of not as a sharp break with the medieval past but, rather, as a time when many movements and ideas originating in the middle ages came to fruition. The later period was thus not so much a time of rebirth as of shifting emphasis, a time when the tempo of human activity quickened and men thought more explicitly about things of this world without reference to the hereafter or without allowing themselves to be quite so influenced by the traditional standards of Christian belief as they had been previously.

In somewhat the same way our understanding of the term "Reformation," as used to describe the period of religious struggle in the 16th century, has also changed. When the division between Catholics and Protestants first occurred, the religious leaders who broke away from the medieval church thought of themselves as "reformers" whose purpose was to eliminate the abuses in the church which, as they saw it, had grown up

EVENTS AND DEFINITIONS

A. The Renaissance, c. 1400-1600

1. Economic and Social Change

A. USE OF NEW FINANCIAL TECHNIQUES. Bills of exchange (drafts calling for the payment of sums of money by one merchant in behalf of another), promissory notes, and discounting (deducting of charges for interest in advance from loans), which greatly expanded credit and eased the transfer of wealth, began to be used extensively from the 14th century onward. Earliest public banks created in the early 15th century. Stock and monetary exchanges *(bourses)* established, the most famous of which was that founded at Antwerp, 1531.

B. DEVELOPMENT OF BUSINESS ORGANIZATION. Double-entry system of bookkeeping in use as early as the 14th century. Permanent business partnerships, group organizations to share insurance risks, and, finally, the joint-stock company evolved from the 14th through the 17th centuries.

C. CHANGING ATTITUDES TOWARD TRADE AND FINANCE. Growth of the "capitalist spirit": from the 14th century onward the search for material wealth and the inherent conditions of economic enterprise in a money economy undermined the prohibitions of the church against the taking of interest (usury) and selling at more than a "just price." In part, this was a reflection of the growing interest in things of this world, of a during the long centuries of papal supremacy. In most cases, they wished not to create something new or to destroy the unity of Christendom by founding numerous sects and denominations but rather to restore the church as it had been founded by Christ and the apostles. For this reason they were driven to appeal to the authority of the Bible as against the authority of the popes and the historical traditions of the church. But because the language of scripture was (and is) in many places ambiguous or even contradictory, they found themselves in disagreement, not only with the medieval church but also among themselves. As a consequence, the great Protestant hope of reforming and preserving a united Christian church was never achieved. The medieval church (thenceforward to be known as the Roman Catholic church) continued to exist side by side with the various new Protestant denominations; and the Reformation, with time, took on the aspects not of a reform movement but of a religious revolution with far-reaching significance.

A. The Renaissance

1. Economic and Social Changes

By the late 14th century the forces of economic expansion, which had begun their work some two or three centuries earlier, had produced a high level of material well-being, particularly in the great European cities. At first this increase in wealth was most noticeable in the Italian peninsula and the Low Countries (now Belgium and Holland), but in time it spread rapidly to other parts of northern and western Europe. As it spread, it created a new, sophisticated, mercantile civilization, outstanding examples of which were the great city-states: Venice, Genoa, Florence, Milan in Italy; Antwerp, Bruges, and Ghent in the Low Countries; and the towns of the Hanseatic League in north central Germany. The most brilliant manifestations of this new civilization were those in Italy, where the continuity of city life from Roman times onward had never been completely broken. In the Italian cities great merchant families made use of their wealth to promote learning and the arts. In so doing, however, they seldom lost sight of the practical side of their affairs; in these Italian merchant communities many of the business skills were developed which were later to be used internationally. For the first time there appeared on the European scene the great financier whose wealth made him the creditor of kings and gave him a power (sometimes exaggerated by later historians) to influence political decisions.

The Renaissance also saw the completion of that process of state de-

desire for well-being in the here and now without awaiting some future life. With the growth of this new spirit and the greater accumulation of commercial and financial wealth, the great merchants and financiers became important figures.

D. NEW MEN OF WEALTH. Three outstanding illustrations of the new financial-mercantile class were: 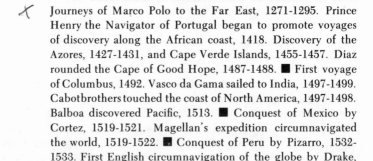 (1) Giovanni dei Medici (1360-1429), merchant and banker of Florence, who founded the powerful Medici family. His descendants later became princes and popes. ■ (2) Jacques Coeur (*c.* 1395-1456), merchant of Bourges in France, possessed the largest fortune ever amassed by a private individual in France down to his time. Friend, confidant, and adviser to French kings. ■ (3) The Fugger family in Germany began to grow in wealth at the end of the 14th century. By the 16th century its members were the wealthiest men in Europe, one of whom supplied the vast sums needed to carry the imperial election of 1519 in favor of Charles of Hapsburg.

2. The Great Discoveries

A. CAUSES. (1) Growth of wealth, which made expensive and risky overseas ventures possible; (2) religious and national zeal; (3) desire for gain; (4) effort of some religious minorities to escape persecution; (5) curiosity and the simple desire to increase knowledge; and, finally, (6) the development of a technology that made long oceanic voyages possible (compass, sternpost rudder, seaworthy construction of ships, improved methods of celestial navigation).

B. CHRONOLOGY OF DISCOVERY AND SETTLEMENT TO 1620. Journeys of Marco Polo to the Far East, 1271-1295. Prince Henry the Navigator of Portugal began to promote voyages of discovery along the African coast, 1418. Discovery of the Azores, 1427-1431, and Cape Verde Islands, 1455-1457. Diaz rounded the Cape of Good Hope, 1487-1488. ■ First voyage of Columbus, 1492. Vasco da Gama sailed to India, 1497-1499. Cabot brothers touched the coast of North America, 1497-1498. Balboa discovered Pacific, 1513. ■ Conquest of Mexico by Cortez, 1519-1521. Magellan's expedition circumnavigated the world, 1519-1522. ■ Conquest of Peru by Pizarro, 1532-1533. First English circumnavigation of the globe by Drake, 1577-1580. Beginning of Dutch trade with the East Indies, 1595-1597. Founding of the English East India Company, velopment begun by medieval kings. Curiously enough, the areas most affected by this change, namely, England, France, and Spain, were not the first to feel the effects of the quickened economic and intellectual tempo. It was in Italy that the new spirit first appeared, but there the Renaissance was a period of political chaos when city fought city and foreign powers intervened to carve out Italian possessions for themselves. In the three aforementioned states, however, the end of the 15th and the beginning of the 16th century saw the emergence of three strong dynasties (Tudors in England, Valois in France, Hapsburgs in Spain) who greatly increased the power of their respective governments and virtually eliminated the last vestiges of feudal opposition. With the rise of these new states the center of European power shifted to the Atlantic fringe, and a new era—the age of the absolute monarchies—had begun.

2. The Great Discoveries

While the important internal changes were taking place in the 15th and 16th centuries, another series of events decisively altered the relations of Europe with the rest of the world and led ultimately to Europe's becoming the center of a worldwide cultural and economic community. These were the great discoveries beyond the seas. Columbus's famous voyage was but one of many and, in its way, only the most sensational of them. The discoveries, and the colonization movements that followed in their wake, were the further result of a number of medieval and Renaissance developments: (1) the internal expansion of European wealth which made it possible to finance costly voyages and to undertake extensive colonization programs; (2) a rise in the level of shipbuilding techniques; (3) improvement in the methods of economic and political organization— e.g. the joint-stock company, which made possible the sharing of great economic risks, and the strong, centralized state which enabled European rulers to give sanction and support to overseas activities; and (4) the growth and improvement of communications within Europe which stimulated interest in remote territories. The motives which drove Europeans to undertake the risks of discovery and exploration were varied. Many were driven by hope of sudden wealth or by the desire to open new trade routes. Some hoped to Christianize the pagans or, later, to escape from religious persecution at home. Kings were moved by considerations of power and prestige. All, however, were impelled by some form of that

1600; of the Dutch East India Company, 1602. ■ English settlement in North America (Jamestown), 1607. Founding of French Canada (Québec) by Champlain, 1608. Establishment of the English in India, 1609-1614. ■ Voyage of the *Mayflower;* second permanent English settlement in North America, 1620-1621.

3. Literature and Thought

A. IN ITALY. *Divine Comedy,* written between 1300 and 1311, while it reflected the ideals of the 13th century also foreshadowed the future since it was written in the vernacular (Italian rather than Latin). The writings of Petrarch (1304-1374) characterized the change; topics chosen were secular in interest. Publication of Boccaccio's *Decameron,* 1353. Founding of the humanist school at Mantua, 1425. Marsilio Ficino became head of the Platonic Academy (whose members opposed the Aristotelian influences of the medieval schoolmen) at Florence, 1458. Rule of Lorenzo de Medici ("the Magnificent") in Florence, 1469-1492. Appearance of Machiavelli's *The Prince,* 1515.

B. OUTSIDE ITALY. Publication of the first part of Cervantes' *Don Quixote* (Spain), 1505. Erasmus' *In Praise of Folly* (1509) satirized contemporary ills, particularly those of the church. Thomas More's *Utopia,* 1516. Foundation of the Collège de France (1530) which became the center of French humanism. Rabelais' *Gargantua and Pantagruel,* 1532. Andreas Vesalius published *Seven Books on the Structure of the Human Body,* 1543. Appearance of Copernicus's *De revolutionibis orbium coelestium (On the Revolution of Celestial Bodies),* 1543. Shakespeare's first plays appeared, 1590-1594. Publication of the first part of Edmund Spenser's *The Faerie Queene,* 1590.

4. Renaissance Art

A. IN ITALY. Giotto's frescoes at Padua, 1305. Botticelli painted "Birth of Venus," 1485. Leonardo da Vinci's "Last Supper" painted, 1485-1498. Construction began on the basil-

restless human vitality and curiosity which has been so marked a characteristic of modern European civilization.

3. Literature and Thought

In the literary movements of the Renaissance two distinctive features
emerged. The first of these was the tendency, already evident in Dante's
Divine Comedy (though, as we have seen, its content was purely medieval), to make use of the native (vernacular) languages rather than medieval Latin as a medium of expression. This change, though it did open
the way to a broadening of interests and tastes, was not all gain, for it
resulted in the decline of an international language which had helped
to unify western Christendom. The second distinctive feature of the new
literature was its emphasis on man and man's place in this world (humanism), stimulated by an interest in the writings of classical antiquity. Because many of the leading literary figures of the early Renaissance, men like
the poet-scholar Petrarch (1304-1374), wished to return to the grammati-
cal purity of classical Latin which medieval Latin had lost, it later came
to be assumed that medieval scholars had known nothing of the great
literary works of antiquity and that the Renaissance scholars, by re-
discovering them, had truly ushered in an age of "rebirth." The claim
was an exaggeration, but it was not entirely without meaning, for Renaissance scholars and thinkers did help to shift both the intellectual and
literary interests of the time from Christian to classical or secular subjects.
With this shift a great number of thinkers began to concern themselves
with man as he is in the world of here and now. Our best illustration of
this new tendency is to be found in the writings of that tough-minded
realist, Niccolo Machiavelli (1469-1527), whose political writings—the most
famous of which was *The Prince*—helped to divorce political theory
from Christian morality. At the other extreme, however, was the Dutch
humanist scholar Erasmus (1466-1536), whose breadth of knowledge
led him to exalt human values but not to separate them from the traditional Christian ethics.

4. Renaissance Art

The art of the Renaissance also reflects the change in emphasis characteristic of its literature and thought. While architecture, as seen in the
great Gothic cathedrals had been the highest artistic achievement of

ica of St. Peter's (Rome), 1506. "School of Athens" and "Disputa" painted by Raphael, 1509-1511. Painting of Michelangelo's "Last Judgment," 1534-1541. Death of Titian, 1576.

B. OUTSIDE ITALY. Albrecht Dürer's woodcuts on "The Revelation of St. John" (Germany), 1498. Hans Holbein the Younger settled in England, 1532. Philibert Delorme published French manual of architecture, 1561. Escorial Palace built by Philip II of Spain at Madrid, 1563-1584. Death of El Greco, 1625, greatest Spanish painter of the Renaissance.

B. The Reformation

John Wyclif (1320-84) of England attacked the theology of the medieval church, 1378-80; Wyclif's followers, known as Lollards, suppressed by King Henry IV (1399-1413). Great schism of the church finally healed by Council of Constance; same council also executed the Bohemian John Hus for heresy, 1415. Restoration of papal unity with election of Martin V, 1517. Hussite Wars in Bohemia, 1420-33. Conciliar movement, which threatened papal authority, finally lost out in struggle with papacy when Council of Basel, 1431-49, failed in its attempt to make a representative council the governing body of the Church. Decline of the Renaissance papacy: pontificate of the humanist pope, Nicholas V, 1447-55; Alexander VI (Borgia), 1492-1503. Establishment of the Spanish Inquisition, 1478. Savonarola preached against clerical abuses at Florence, 1494-98. Humanist criticism of clerical abuses: *In Praise of Folly* by Erasmus, 1509; *Utopia* by Sir Thomas More, 1516; *The Letters of Obscure Men* by Rubeanus and Ulrich von Hutten, 1515-17.

Influence of humanism on the Reformation: Although humanist criticism had much to do with preparing the climate of opinion that made the Reformation possible, humanism and Protestantism were separate and distinct movements. Humanist critics, particularly in northern Europe, were not anti-Christian or even opposed to the medieval Church as it was constituted about 1500. Most of them, when the crisis of the Reformation came, remained within the Church. Their writings and attitudes, however, inadvertently made men aware of medieval man, in contrast, the Renaissance artist turned his attention to such individual forms of art as painting and sculpture. As a consequence of a revolution in artistic method, the new artist was able to portray his subjects with a natural exactness and a richness of detail that had been lacking in medieval art; and while he still chose religious themes for expression, he also chose many that were nonreligious. The growth of artistic naturalism may be traced from its beginnings in Giotto's (*c.* 1270-1337) paintings through the pictures and sculpture of such great figures as Leonardo da Vinci (1452-1519), Michelangelo (1475-1564), and Titian (1477-1576), whose work typifies the new diversity and variety of a vastly enriched artistic medium.

B. The Reformation

When we look for the general causes of the great religious split between Catholics and Protestants, which began with Martin Luther (1483-1546) in the first quarter of the 16th century, we find two kinds.

The first type arose from the great changes in the attitude of men toward the world in which they lived, that had occurred during the 14th, 15th, and 16th centuries. These changes were bound to make many persons resentful of an authority like that of the medieval church, which professed to be universal and supernatural. Kings and nobles disliked the moral curbs placed on them by the church's teachings and looked with disfavor and envy on the growing wealth and the administrative bureaucracy of such a powerful organization. Merchants were restive at the traditional prohibitions of canon law against the taking of interest on loans and against other business practices that are now accepted as normal and honorable, even though these prohibitions had declined in force during the late middle ages. Moreover, with the rise of strong monarchies and the growth of a sense of national distinctiveness, it was difficult for many Europeans to think of the papacy as anything other than an Italian institution which drew taxes from them to serve its own ends. In the face of these growing forces of secular discontent, it is probable that some sort of break with papal authority might have come without a Martin Luther to cause it. Attitudes had changed and the changes led men more and more to a rejection of the church's spiritual teachings.

The second variety of general cause of the Reformation lay in the Renaissance church itself, which gave Luther and other Protestants something to criticize and thus helped to create the upheaval that followed. For the fact was that some of the churchmen, though by no means all or even a majority, had succumbed to the secular influences of the age. Ecclesiastical the Church's shortcomings in the early 16th century. Concordat of Bologna between papacy and Francis I of France gave the king virtual control of the French Church; publication of new Greek edition of the New Testament by Erasmus; indulgence mission of Tetzel to Germany, 1516. Reign of the Emperor Charles V, 1519-1556.

1. Lutheranism

Luther's life: born at Eisleben, 1483. Studied at University of Erfurt whose leading theologian, Gabriel Biel (d. 1495), was under the influence of the "nominalist" philosopher William of Ockham (c. 1300-49). Like most Ockhamists, Luther believed in the separation of reason and faith. Entered the order of Augustinian Eremites, 1505; ordained priest, 1507. Visited Rome, 1510-11, and taught at Wittenberg after 1512. Gradually came to conclusion that man is "justified by faith alone," 1512-1517. In reaction to the Tetzel indulgence mission published his 95 Theses, 1517. Excommunicated by Pope Leo X, 1520. Defied Emperor Charles V at Diet of Worms, 1521. Took the side of the princes in suppressing Peasants' Revolt, 1524-25. Later history of Lutheranism: Augsburg Confession (*Confessio Augustana*) set forth principles of Lutheran belief, 1531. National Protestant (Lutheran) church established in Sweden, 1527; in Denmark, 1536. Lutheran-Catholic religious wars (1546-55) culminated in Peace of Augsburg, 1555, which recognized Lutheranism; permitted princes to determine which faith would prevail in their territories ("cuius regio, eius religio").

2. Calvinism

Translation of the Bible into French, 1523-1530. Calvin converted to Protestantism and fled Paris, 1533. Publication of Calvin's *Institutes of the Christian Religion*, 1536. Founding of theocratic Calvinist state at Geneva, 1541. British exiles carry Calvinist ideas to England (after the accession of Elizabeth I in 1558) and Scotland (John Knox returned in 1559). Scottish parliament severed ties with Rome, 1560. Death of Calvin, 1564. Revolt of the Netherlands begun in part under Calvinist auspices, 1566. Declaration of Dutch independence from Spain, 1581. Religious Wars in France (Catholics against discipline and morality had become lax in many places, and, what was worse, some of the Renaissance popes themselves were guilty of flagrant abuses of their high office. Thus a combination of discontents came into existence, some aroused by secular feelings and others by a fear that the church, through certain of its practices, was placing the salvation of thousands of human beings in jeopardy. For men like Martin Luther and John Calvin (1509-1564), who were destined to become the two leading figures of the Protestant movement, the latter issue was by far the most important. Though there were men who would follow their lead for selfish, material reasons, these two acted on the high religious purpose of restoring the church of the apostles.

1. Lutheranism

In 1517, Luther initiated the religious revolt in Germany with a public challenge (Ninety-five Theses) to debate certain propositions which struck at the heart of the prevailing theology of the church and implicitly questioned papal authority. His challenge struck a chord of popular response and within a few years had led to his expulsion from the church. What made it possible for Luther to succeed where earlier religious leaders had failed was the decision on the part of certain territorial princes and nobles to back him in his struggle. This support left the lands of the Holy Roman Empire divided into two armed camps. On one side were the Lutheran nobles and on the other the Emperor Charles V (1519-1556), who remained loyal to the Roman Catholic church. After a period of protracted warfare in which the two sides fought each other to a standstill, the Peace of Augsburg (1555) effected a compromise by allowing local princes to determine what the religions of their territories would be. With this adjustment, Protestantism became a permanent part of the European historical tradition.

2. Calvinism

While Lutheranism spread throughout north Germany and into Scandinavia, elsewhere in Europe a new and equally strong protest movement was also taking shape. In Switzerland, where the religious leader Ulrich Zwingli had begun the revolt of 1524, a new and powerful personality— John Calvin, a French preacher of the new doctrines who had fled to the city of Geneva in 1536—undertook to organize the church which afterwards bore his name. The distinctiveness of the Calvinist church organization lay in the fact that it allowed the laity to participate in church functions as members of the governing body known as the "presbytery." Above the presbytery was a hierarchy of graded courts which undertook the surveilthe Calvinist Huguenots), 1563-1598: massacre of St. Bartholomew wiped out important French Huguenot leaders, 1572; Henry IV became Catholic convert from Calvinism, 1593, and issued the Edict of Nantes granting toleration to Huguenots, 1598.

3. Anglicanism

Henry VIII (1509-1547) summoned the Reformation Parliament, 1529. Henry divorced Catherine of Aragon and married Anne Boleyn, 1533; Pope Clement VII excommunicated Henry. Henry proclaimed head of the Church of England, 1534. Dissolution of the monasteries, 1536-1539. Protestant reforms pushed under Edward VI (1547-1553); first English Book of Common Prayer published, 1549. Catholicism restored during the reign of Queen Mary, 1553-1558. Queen Elizabeth I (1558-1603) established Anglican church: Act of Supremacy recognized queen's control of the church and Act of Uniformity (both in 1559) ordered Englishmen to conform to the new ceremonies. Thirty-nine Articles (1563) defined the theology of the Church of England.

English Puritans began to protest against vestiges of medieval customs in the English Church after 1566. Richard Hooker wrote the *Laws of Ecclesiastical Polity* which defined the theological position of Anglicanism, 1594-1601. James I (1603-25) rejected Puritan demands for reform at Hampton Court Conference, 1604.

lance of public morality with far greater efficiency than any the courts of the medieval church had possessed. From the outset Calvin made it plain that his movement was intended to supplant the medieval church, to become, in other words, the universal, "reformed" church of Christendom. Impelled by this purpose, Calvinism spread rapidly into France, the Low Countries, the Holy Roman Empire, Scotland, and England. Wherever it appeared, the militancy of its adherents frequently led to conflicts with the existing authority and in some countries to bitter wars of religion.

3. Anglicanism

Anglican Protestantism, that branch of the new movement which developed the English state church, differed from Lutheranism and Calvinism in that the original leadership of the revolt did not come from a great religious leader (though many prominent churchmen gave it their support) but from the state. King Henry VIII (1509-1547) broke with papal authority and proclaimed himself head of the Church of England in 1534. His motives were complex—personal, political, dynastic, patriotic, and vaguely reformist. At first, this break took the form of a schism (separation) in which all the forms, ceremonies, and much of the theology of the medieval church were preserved. Gradually, however, as Henry moved to abolish the monasteries and to introduce other changes, the English church became more and more Protestant. In the reign of Edward VI (1547-1553) the Protestantizing of the church was accelerated with such success that the efforts of the Catholic Queen Mary (1553-1558) to restore England to her own faith proved unavailing. With the accession of Elizabeth I (1558-1603) the form of the Anglican church was finally settled by a compromise in which the organization of the medieval church was retained but the theology of continental Protestantism became the basis of doctrinal belief. Unfortunately, though many Englishmen were satisfied with this middle-of-the-road position, others were not, and this discontent sowed the seeds of later trouble. Catholics disliked the Church of England's theology and its denial of papal authority, whereas the Puritans, a new group so known from their wish to "purify" the church, were angry at its retention of certain Catholic elements. In spite of these difficulties, the Anglican church, because it was purposely broad and comprehensive in its doctrines, was able to include in its membership the great body of loyal Englishmen. In this way it became the prototype of the new kind of "national church that sprang up all over Europe in the wake of the Reformation."

4. The Catholic Reformation

Founding of the Theatine (1524) and Capuchin (1525-1528) orders for the purpose of reforming clerical life. Society of Jesus (Jesuits) organized by Ignatius Loyola (1534); recognized by the pope, 1540. The order was intended through its militancy and discipline to win back Protestants and to combat heresy. Council of Trent reaffirmed the doctrinal position of the church and pronounced the various Protestant theologies to be heresies; undertook extensive reforms in clerical life, 1545-1563. Reform of the Roman curia (central governing body of the Catholic Church) by Pope Paul IV, 1555-1559. Index of prohibited books established, 1557.

5. The Historical Significance of Protestantism

(a) Major Religious Divisions of Europe after the Reformation. (E in parentheses denotes established or official state churches.)

(1) Lutheran:
North Germany: Hesse (E), Saxony (E), Brandenburg (Prussia) (E), Württemberg (E).
Scandinavia: Denmark (E), Norway (E), Sweden (E), Finland (E).

(2) Calvinism:
Rhenish Palatinate (E), parts of Hungary and Poland, regions of western and southwestern France, parts of north Germany, the Netherlands (E), Scotland (E), parts of England, northern Ireland, Geneva (E), and parts of Switzerland.

(3) Anglicanism:
England and Wales (E); established church in Ireland though the great majority of the population remained Catholic.

4. The Catholic Reformation

In the face of growing religious unrest which threatened, by the middle of the 16th century, to destroy the medieval church completely, a series of movements was begun within the Catholic church to strengthen its organization and to eliminate some of the things that had brought on the Protestant revolt. Moves to counter the various outbreaks of religious rebellion sometimes took the form of repression. The Inquisition, a special administrative body originally organized in the middle ages for the examination of heretics, was given wide powers, particularly in Spain and Italy, while the support of Catholic kings and nobles was solicited to prevent the further spread of heresy. The greatest successes of the church, however, were achieved as a result of a spiritual rejuvenation in which the Society of Jesus (Jesuits), founded in 1540 by the soldier-saint Ignatius Loyola (1491-1556), took the lead. By stressing discipline, loyalty to the papacy, and a firm adherence to both religious principles and intellectual standards, the Jesuits were able to keep and to win back countless numbers for the church. In the climax a great church council held at Trent in Italy (1545-1563) reaffirmed the doctrinal teachings of the church; and while this orthodox body prevented any final reconciliation with the Protestants, it reformed numerous things that had been complained of and restored the high standards of Catholic clerical life.

5. The Historical Significance of Protestantism

Protestantism has sometimes been looked upon by historians as the source of many such modern developments as capitalism, liberalism, democracy, and nationalism. In the main, this conclusion has derived from the belief that Protestantism, and particularly Calvinism, by its stress on scriptural authority and through its theology, opened the way to a philosophy of individualism which greatly influenced modern economic and political thinking. This view is sound only if we look at certain indirect effects of Protestant thought. Both Luther and Calvin rejected the doctrine implicit in medieval theology that men could win their salvation through any merits (good works) of their own. Men were saved, they held, because God willed that they should be saved and not through any ministrations or sacraments of the church. In other words, salvation was given to men because they had faith in God and not because they did good in the world. The major Protestant theologians stressed this view because they felt that the medieval church had placed too much stress on certain practices which made it seem that men could buy their way into heaven. In thus arguing, however, leading Protestant thinkers had to face up to a dilemma. If men were saved by faith alone, then what incentive was there for human beings to live decent, moral lives? This problem Calvin felt he had solved

      (4) Roman Catholic:
          Poland, most of Hungary, south Germany, Austria, France, Spain, Portugal, the Italian peninsula. Where the Roman Catholic Church survived it was invariably the established church.

(b) Other Religious Movements.

      (1) English Puritanism originated c. 1566 as a movement to "purify" the Church of England.

      (2) Socinianism, forerunner of later Unitarianism, founded by Laelius (1525-62) and Faustus (1539-1604) Socinus (Sozzini), two 16th-century Italian reformers.

      (3) Separatism: term applied to those English Puritan groups after 1588 who wished to "separate" from the Church of England rather than to reform it from within.

      (4) Arminianism: movement within Calvinism named for the Dutch theologian Jacobus Arminius (1560-1609) who sought to mitigate the extreme predestinarian theories of orthodox Calvinism.

      (5) Jansenism: mainly a French movement within the Roman Catholic Church which, like orthodox Calvinism, tended to stress predestination. Took its name from the Dutch Catholic theologian, Bishop Cornelis Jansen (1585-1638), whose posthumous work *Augustinus* (1643) became the theological basis of the movement.

      (6) English-speaking denominationalism: one of the extraordinary characteristics of English Protestantism was its tendency to divide into numerous denominations. Among the more famous of these were: the Independents (Congregationalists), whose leading members were the poet John Milton, Oliver Cromwell, and the New England theologian John Cotton; the General Baptists, believed to have been founded by the English nonconformist clergyman John Smyth in 1611; the Quakers founded by George Fox (1624-91) about 1647.

when he argued that those who possessed faith and were truly among the "elect" chosen for salvation could not be immoral. On the contrary, because they were saved, they would "demonstrate their election" by their austerity, self-denial, and personal morality. This theory, some historians have contended, led the Calvinist to an extreme emphasis on individual morality that made him a hard-working, frugal, productive member of society. Because these virtues are conducive to the accumulation of wealth, it has also been argued that Calvinism was a religion peculiarly favorable to the development of modern capitalism. In this sense, there may be an element of truth to the argument, though it does not take into consideration one or two important facts: first, that such virtues are not always peculiar to Protestant or, specifically, Calvinist societies; and second, that in their social thinking and attitudes the Catholics and Protestants of the 16th and 17th centuries shared many views.

In somewhat the same way it has been said that Protestantism was largely responsible for modern liberalism and democracy because it promoted religious toleration, emphasized religious individualism, and among some sects, used the forms of representative government. Again, such arguments may have some validity if we recognize that these results were quite indirect and inadvertent. At their inception many of the larger Protestant denominations were not believers in religious toleration and, in many cases, came round to it only when it was clear that their own churches were not going to supplant all others. Nor were Protestants, over all, believers in democracy, any more than most people in the 16th and 17th centuries. Like most other Europeans of the period, they would have been horrified at the modern democratic state.

In one important area, but again indirectly, Protestantism seems to have had a significant effect, though even this one should not be exaggerated. This was the influence of Protestantism on the rise of modern nationalism. Some, but by no means all, of the Protestant churches, and particularly those which, like the Church of England, became state-supported or established institutions, tended to unite patriotism and denominationalism by coming under the control of the state. In this way, though it was usually not their intention to do so, they helped to destroy the older, organized unity of Christendom which had been one of the major characteristics of medieval civilization.

After all, it should not be forgotten that Protestantism, whatever its social or political effects, was still a religious movement concerned with religious aims and purposes. We should be careful not to read backward into it (or other historical movements for that matter) ideas and attitudes which were completely alien to its point of view.

EVENTS AND DEFINITIONS

Leading European Dynasties, 1500-1800.
(a) England (after 1603 known as Great Britain).
  (1) The Tudors, 1485-1603.
    Henry VII, 1485-1509; Henry VIII, 1509-1547; Edward VI, 1547-1553; Mary, 1553-1558; Elizabeth I, 1558-1603.

CHAPTER 8

The Age of the Absolute Monarchies

THE ESSENTIAL MOVEMENT

The period from the 16th through the 18th centuries was a time when most of the nations of modern Europe took the form in which we know them today. In almost every major western country the power of the king had grown to a point where those other elements in society, viz., the feudal nobility and the church, which had formerly acted as checks on royal authority, were now either completely broken or else absorbed into the royal administration. There were, of course, exceptions to this pattern of development, most notably England, where the power of the crown was drastically curbed by the end of the 17th century, but, in the main, the 300 years lying between 1500 and 1800 saw the monarchs of Europe victorious in the extension of their power and authority. As we have seen, European kings from the middle ages onward had come more and more to symbolize the new, impersonal nation-state. The king's law, the civil administration, the standing army were all instruments of a new kind of statecraft which, while they were employed to serve the interests of the prince, were also intended to serve the society over which the crown had absolute power. This was the ideal of absolute monarchy and in the degree that it approached this ideal it was successful in maintaining itself. Unfortunately, however, this kind of state had several great weaknesses which, in the end, wrought its undoing. First, its efficiency and impartiality depended not only upon a bureaucracy (whose members often entrenched themselves in offices which were bought and sold

(2) The Stuarts, 1603-1714.

James VI (of Scotland) became James I of England, 1603-25; Charles I, 1625-49; Interregnum (rule of the army leaders, most important of whom was Oliver Cromwell, d. 1658), 1649-60; Charles II, 1660-85; James II, 1685-88; William and Mary, 1688-1702; Anne, 1702-14.

(3) The Hanoverians (House of Brunswick).

George I, 1714-27; George II, 1727-60; George III, 1760-1820.

(b) France.

(1) Valois kings.

Charles VIII, 1498-1515; Francis I, 1515-47; Henry II, 1547-59; Francis II, 1559-60; Charles IX, 1560-74; Henry III, 1574-89.

(2) Bourbon kings.

Henry IV, 1589-1610; Louis XIII, 1610-43; Louis XIV, 1643-1715; Louis XV, 1715-74; Louis XVI, 1774-92.

(c) Holy Roman Empire (House of Hapsburg).

Maximilian I, 1493-1519; Charles V, 1519-56; Ferdinand I, 1556-64; Maximilian II, 1564-76; Rudolf II, 1576-1612; Mathias, 1612-19; Ferdinand II, 1619-37; Ferdinand III, 1637-57; Leopold I, 1658-1705; Joseph I, 1705-11; Charles VI, 1711-40; Francis I (of Lorraine), 1745-65, and Maria Theresa, 1740-1780; Joseph II, 1765-90; Leopold II, 1790-92; Francis II (took title of Francis I of Austria after 1806), 1792-1835.

(d) Russia (Romanovs).

Michael, 1613-45; Alexis, 1645-76; Theodore III, 1676-82; Ivan V, 1682-89; Peter I (the Great), 1689-1725; Catherine I, 1725-27; Peter II, 1727-30; Anna, 1730-40; Elizabeth, 1741-62; Peter III, 1762; Catherine II (the Great), 1762-96; Paul I, 1796-1801.

(e) Prussia (Hohenzollerns).

Frederick William (the Great Elector), 1640-88; Frederick I (first Prussian king), 1688-1713; Frederick William I, 1713-40; Frederick II (the Great), 1740-86; Frederick William II, 1786-97; Frederick William III, 1797-1840.

or passed from father to son) but also upon the personal abilities of a sovereign (whose qualities as a ruler, because of the uncertainties of dynastic inheritance, varied greatly from generation to generation). Second, though western European kings were to some extent limited in their absolute freedom to make political decisions, there was nothing short of rebellion or military defeat by a neighboring state which could keep them from carrying out policies that were sometimes dangerous to the welfare of their subjects. And, third, while the absolute monarchy did a great deal to destroy the powers and privileges of the nobility, it did not erase them entirely and, in some cases, actually increased them so long as the nobles were willing to become the servants and supporters of the state. These three weaknesses, coupled with rising costs of government from the 16th century onward, created a number of complex problems with which absolute governments were less and less able to cope successfully.

A. Dynastic Conflicts and Wars of Religion

In the period between 1500 and 1715, the territorial and dynastic ambitions of the various European states led to an almost incessant warfare which gave the ascendancy first to one power or group of powers and then to another. These contests were not simply straightforward struggles for lands and power but were complicated by the religious divisions of the Reformation. Just as there were Catholic and Protestant parties which fought savage civil wars in many countries, so, too, there were Catholic and Protestant nations whose interests divided the whole of Europe into armed camps. In time, however, while religious motives were occasionally strong enough to sway the policies of particular rulers or countries, other considerations, more mundane, came to have an increasing effect on national policies. By the end of the 16th century it was already possible to observe the rather frequent crossing of religious lines in order to form alliances. A generation later, with the coming of the Thirty Years' War, such practices were quite common. Nonetheless, in spite of the decline of religious partisanship as a cause of wars, many conflicts were greatly intensified when religious zeal coincided with other motives. This was one of the major reasons why the wars of the period from 1500 to 1715 were often fought with an unexampled bitterness that did not subside until after the signing of the Peace of Westphalia in 1648.

Let us now look briefly at the role of several of the more important states in the international affairs of this troubled period.

A. Dynastic Conflicts and Wars of Religion

1. Spain

Reign of Ferdinand and Isabella (1479-1516) saw the union of Castile and Aragon, the downfall of the last Moorish state, and the beginning of Spanish overseas expansion. Charles I (of Spain) became king (1516-1556) and Holy Roman Emperor as Charles V, 1519-1556. Hapsburg-Valois rivalry led to wars with France: 1521-1529; 1535-1538; 1542-1545; 1551-1559; which ended with the Treaty of Cateau-Cambrésis—a Spanish triumph that marked the high point of Spanish influence in Europe.

Philip II (1556-1598) committed Spain to the cause of the Catholic Reformation: (1) revolt of the Netherlands, 1568-1609; (2) attempt to invade England—defeat of the Spanish Armada, 1588; (3) intervention in French Wars of Religion, 1589-1598.

Spain entered the Thirty Years' War (1618-1648) on the side of the Austrian Hapsburgs against France. Defeat of the Spanish army by French at Rocroi, 1643, marked the end of Spanish military supremacy in Europe. Treaty of the Pyrenees (1659) signalized the decline of Spain and the rise of France.

Reign of Charles II, 1665-1700, last of the Spanish Hapsburgs. To avoid controversy over succession England, Holland, and France undertook to dispose of Spain and its empire by private agreement, 1698. King Charles, in anger, left his throne to Philip of Anjou, grandson of Louis XIV of France. Austria, England, and Holland formed the Grand Alliance, 1701, to prevent possible union of French and Spanish crowns. War of Spanish Succession, 1701-14.

2. France

Reign of Francis I (1515-1547) marked by the so-called Hapsburg-Valois Wars (see Spain above) and beginning of Protestant movement in France. Treaty of Cateau-Cambrésis (see Spain above), 1559. Wars of Religion, 1563-1598 (see Calvinism, chapter VI). Reign of Henry IV (1589-1610) marked by restoration of strong monarchy and granting of toleration to Huguenots (Edict of Nantes, 1598).

1. Spain

The 16th century was the era of Spain's greatest power. By the year 1500 a number of smaller kingdoms in the Iberian Peninsula had been consolidated under two rulers, Ferdinand and Isabella, who had destroyed the last vestiges of the ancient Islamic power and embarked on an ambitious program of overseas exploration and colonization which was destined to bring wealth and greatness to the newly unified Spanish kingdom. Through intermarriage, the crowns of Spain and the Holy Roman Empire came into the possession of a single dynasty (Hapsburgs), whose leading representative, the Emperor Charles V, was the most powerful ruler of the 16th century. Even so, Charles, a devout Catholic, was not able to check the rise of Lutheranism in Germany. Neither could he entirely eliminate the danger to his family territories arising out of his long rivalry with France. Nevertheless, Charles at his abdication was able to leave to his son, who became Philip II of Spain (1556-1598), a rich inheritance of lands and power. Philip, who was the epitome of the hard-working absolute monarch, at once embarked on a series of projects which were to weaken Spain permanently. All vestiges of religious dissent were ruthlessly suppressed in his dominions. Spanish commerce and industry were rigorously controlled. The military strength of Spain was committed to the cause of the Catholic Reformation and to the weakening of the French monarchy. Philip's most disastrous policies led to a protracted rebellion in the Low Countries, by which Holland finally won its independence, and also to an unsuccessful attempt to conquer England which failed with the defeat of the Spanish armada by the English in 1588. The last years of Philip's life ended in defeat at the hands of the resurgent French monarchy. From these disasters Spain never recovered, though she was to remain a major force in European politics during the first half of the 17th century. By the year 1700 the Spanish kingdom had sunk to the level of a second-rate power.

2. France

The French monarchy, after many vicissitudes which saw it decline from a peak of greatness in the 13th century to the low point of English conquest during the Hundred Years' War (1338-1453), emerged at the end of the 15th century as one of the strong states of Europe. With the accession of Francis I (1515-1547) the long rivalry between the French kings and the Hapsburgs, which was to influence European international relations for more than two centuries, was begun. Despite

LouisXIII (1610-1643) made Cardinal Richelieu (in power from 1624 to 1642) his chief adviser. The latter (1) broke the independent power of the Huguenots, (2) strengthened the monarchy by checking the feudal nobles, and (3) curbed the House of Hapsburg by intervening in the Thirty Years' War on the side of the German Protestants (1635-1648).

Reign of Louis XIV (1643-1715) saw the emergence of France as the leading power of Europe. Treaty of the Pyrenees, 1659 (see Spain above). Colbert as Controller-General of Finances (1662-1683) stimulated French economic growth and created the system of mercantilism in its classic form (see p. 37, text). Wars of Devolution, 1667-1668 (over the Spanish Netherlands); 1672-1678 (against Holland). Revocation of the Edict of Nantes (1685) forced thousands of Huguenots into exile. War of the League of Augsburg (over the Rhenish Palatinate), 1688-1697. War of the Spanish Succession (over uniting the crowns of Spain and France), 1701-1714. Treaties of Utrecht (1713) and Rastadt (1714) provided that Louis XIV's grandson Philip V should remain on the Spanish throne but that France and Spain should never be unified. Death of Louis XIV (1715) left France severely strained in finances and manpower. Louis XV, 1715-74, great-grandson of Louis XIV, succeeded. "Mississippi Bubble," 1718-20, caused by speculation promoted by the financier John Law. France participated in the War of the Polish Succession in alliance with Spain and Sardinia, 1733-38. War of the Austrian Succession in which France allied with Prussia supported the Bavarian elector's claims to the Holy Roman Empire against Maria Theresa, 1740-48. "Diplomatic Revolution" saw France allied with the Hapsburgs for the first time in history in the ensuing Seven Years' War, 1756-63.

3. England

Reign of Henry VII (1485-1509); order restored after the Wars of the Roses; monarchy strengthened; Court of Star Chamber established, 1487. Reign of Henry VIII (1509-1547) chancellorship of Cardinal Wolsey, 1515-1529; Act of Supremacy made Henry head of the English Church, 1534 (for other changes see Anglicanism, chapter VI).

his incessant wars, Francis strengthened the monarchy and during the period of religious upheaval kept France firmly Catholic although a large segment of the French population was won over to Calvinism. In the reign of his grandson, Charles IX, a series of civil wars began between Catholics and Huguenots (Protestants) which lasted to the end of the 16th century. These were not terminated until the former Protestant prince, Henry IV (1589-1610), issued the Edict of Nantes (1598) granting religious toleration and a measure of security to the Huguenots.

Under Henry and his successors, Louis XIII (1610-1643) and Louis XIV (1643-1715), both the French state and French society underwent a process of reconstruction after the long period of religious struggle. As a consequence, France emerged during the last half of the 17th century as the leading nation of Europe. The architects of this reconstruction were Cardinal Richelieu (1585-1642) under Louis XIII, and Cardinal Mazarin (1602-1661) under Louis XIV. Through their efforts the royal government was made transcendent over French localism and various elements (Huguenots and nobles) potentially dangerous to the state were deprived of any further power to do harm. Withal, the state did its best to strengthen the economy through the protection of French manufactures and the strict regulation of foreign trade. This policy, known as mercantilism, was fully developed and put into practice by Colbert (1619-1683), the finance minister of Louis XIV. The work of these three men enabled King Louis to embark on that series of expansionist wars at the end of the 17th century which, while they made France feared throughout Europe, disastrously weakened the internal structure of French society and dissipated its laboriously accumulated wealth.

In spite of the unfortunate foreign policy of Louis, the late 17th century was one of the brilliant periods of French history. Cultivated persons everywhere looked to France for cultural inspiration, and the French language became a second tongue for the social and intellectual elites of Europe. This, too, was a great era of French literature which produced such names as Corneille (1606-1684), Molière (1622-1673), and Racine (1639-1699).

3.   England

The history of the English monarchy during the 16th and 17th centuries was, in its conclusion, quite different from that of France or Spain. For more than 150 years, however— from 1485 to 1640—it looked as though England, too, would go the way of most other western European states and become permanently an absolute monarchy. Under the strong Tudor dynasty, whose leading representatives were Henry VII

Reign of Elizabeth I (1558-1603): defeat of the Spanish Armada, 1588; "Golden Age" of English literature.

Reign of James I (1603-1625): conflict with parliament over finances and extension of royal power, 1604-1624.

Reign of Charles I (1625-1649): Petition of Right, 1628; dissolution of parliament and eleven years of personal rule, 1629-1640; Scottish rebellion (1637-1640) forced Charles to call the Long Parliament in 1640; civil wars, 1642-1649; execution of Charles I, 1649.

Commonwealth and Protectorate, 1649-1660: Commonwealth (republic) supplanted the monarchy, 1649-1653; Oliver Cromwell (1599-1658) assumed title of Lord Protector, 1653-1658.

Restoration of the monarchy (1660); reign of Charles II, 1660-1685: Clarendon Code (for the suppression of Protestant dissenters who were not members of the Church of England) formulated, 1661-1665; Charles II and parliament in conflict over the right of his Catholic brother James to succeed to the throne, 1679-1681; Charles attacked the leaders of the Whig party (which favored religious toleration and limited monarchy) and tried to re-establish absolute rule in England, 1681-1685.

Reign of James II (last Catholic king of England), 1685-1688: James attempted to re-establish the Catholic faith and provoked the "Glorious Revolution" of 1688.

Reign of Mary II with William III (of Orange), who had been invited to the English throne, 1689-1702: Bill of Rights, 1689, permanently limited royal power; Act of Settlement, 1701, reserved the English throne for Protestants.

Reign of Anne, 1702-1714: union of England with Scotland, 1707; Peace of Utrecht (1713) saw England's emergence as the leading maritime power of Europe.

Reign of George I (formerly ruler of the small German state of Hanover), 1714-1727: beginning of modern cabinet government under Sir Robert Walpole, first prime minister of England, 1721-1742.

George II, 1727-60, continued Walpole in office. War of Jenkins' Ear with Spain, 1739-48; England participated in the War of the Austrian Succession from 1744-48 as an ally of Austria. Second Jacobite Rebellion, known as "The Forty-five," attempted to place the Stuart pretender, Charles Ed-

(1485-1509), Henry VIII (1509-1547), and Elizabeth I (1558-1603), every tendency pointed in that direction. By reducing the English nobility to obedience, assuming the headship of the church, and reorganizing the machinery of government, these monarchs gave to England a state with all the characteristics of the new kind of monarchy. Though less popular and less able than their Tudor successors, the first two kings of the house of Stuart, James I (1603-1625) and Charles I (1625-1649), tried to carry on with these developments but met disaster in the attempt. In the middle of the 17th century the growth of royal absolutism was suddenly checked by the outbreak of civil war. After a long period of intermittent struggle, which saw the monarchy temporarily replaced by a military dictatorship under Oliver Cromwell (1649-1658), the power of the crown was conclusively curbed by the "Glorious Revolution" of 1688.

Though there are many reasons for England's divergence from the general European pattern of political development, one of the most important was the result of a peculiarly English historical happenstance. England, unlike the continental states, had not only preserved its medieval representative body, the parliament, but had seen that body grow in strength until it had become an integral part of the English system of government. Theoretically, even so late as the 17th century, parliament was not an independent political body representing the will of the people but a dependent institution which the king might merely consult in public matters and which he did not have to call into existence at all if he did not wish to. Because the problem of government finance had become serious by the 17th century, the king was forced to resort to parliament more and more often for financial aid. This aid parliament would give him only at the price of his surrendering some of his powers. When in the end Charles I, in desperation, tried to rule without parliament entirely, his expedient helped to bring on civil war. For Charles, in so doing, challenged a number of discontented groups who were strongly represented in parliament. These were the country gentlemen (gentry), lawyers, merchants, and the various religious groups who were called Puritans. These groups spearheaded the opposition to the crown and, throughout the century, continually tried to hold its power in check.

With the Revolution of 1688, England did not become at once either a democracy or a constitutional monarchy in the modern sense. What it did become was a state in which the final constitutional power was controlled by a rather limited elite of great landholding nobles and gentlemen and a few wealthy merchants who were strong enough to make their influence felt in parliament. Though the English electoral system was to remain thoroughly unrepresentative until drastically reward ("Bonnie Prince Charlie"), on the British throne; rebels decisively defeated at Culloden, 1745-46. Seven Years' War between England and France, 1756-63. Great war ministry of William Pitt the Elder led England to victory, 1757-61. Reign of George III, 1760-1820. Peace of Paris terminated war, 1763.

4. The Holy Roman Empire

Reign of Charles V. (1519-1556): abdication of Charles permanently separated Spain and the Empire under two separate branches of the Hapsburg family.

A. THE THIRTY YEARS' WAR, 1618-1648. Growing religious rivalry within the empire (among Catholics, Lutherans, and Calvinists) led to Thirty Years' War, 1618-1648, which passed through four major phases: (1) the Bohemian period, 1618-1625, when the Bohemians, who had rejected the Emperor Ferdinand II as their ruler and elected Frederick V, a Calvinist and elector of the Rhenish Palatinate, as their king, were defeated by the imperial armies; (2) the Danish period, 1625-1629, when Christian IV of Denmark intervened in the war and was forced to withdraw after defeats by the imperial armies; (3) the Swedish period, 1630-1635, when the Swedish king, Gustavus Adolphus, invaded Germany and was everywhere victorious over the imperialists until his death at the Battle of Lützen in 1632; (4) the Swedish-French period, formed in the 19th century, the revolution engineered by this small aristocratic oligarchy of Englishmen in 1688 was not without great historical significance. Not only did it become the model which justified later revolutions, including those in America and France, but it helped to preserve the traditions of parliamentary government at a moment when they were rapidly disappearing in other parts of Europe.

In other ways, too, the history of England during the 16th and 17th centuries was marked by developments of importance to the western world. This was a remarkable era of English intellectual and social vitality which had its beginnings in one of the great periods of the world's history, the "Golden Age" of Queen Elizabeth. English seamen, like Drake and Hawkins, pushed into seas previously unknown to England and destroyed the seapower of Spain with their daring. A generation after the defeat of the Spanish armada in 1588 the first English settlements were made in North America. With these events the whole of the western hemisphere came under European colonization and was thus destined to become a part of the larger community of western civilization. In literature, Shakespeare (1564-1616), Spenser (1552?-1599), and Milton (1608-1674) stand out amid a cluster of others that helped to make this one of the major epochs in the history of English writing, for each of these was to have an influence reaching far beyond his native land.

4. The Holy Roman Empire

By 1500, the Holy Roman Empire, which was originally intended to be the proud successor of the first Roman Empire, had become a loose confederation made up largely of small German-speaking principalities who acknowledged the rule of the Hapsburgs as nominally elected emperors. Unlike France or England, the Empire had never developed a centralized government, and the rise of Lutheranism and Calvinism furthered its disunity by dividing the Catholic emperors from their large body of Protestant subjects. In the first quarter of the 17th century, tension between the two camps finally led to the outbreak of a long and unhappy war. This struggle, known as the Thirty Years' War (1618-1648), was more than just a religious conflict. At stake also was the question of imperial authority. If the emperor could make himself master of a strong, unified empire whose princes were dependent directly upon his rule, then the old Holy Roman Empire might well become the most powerful state in Europe. It was in fear of this eventuality, as well as for religious reasons, that other European states came to be involved in the struggle. Before it was finished, at one time or another, England, the Netherlands,

1635-1648, when Sweden and France in alliance carried on the war against the Holy Roman Emperor.

B. PEACE OF WESTPHALIA, 1648. After long war which resulted in serious losses of men and wealth throughout Germany, both sides finally negotiated the Peace of Westphalia, 1648. By its terms the power of the Holy Roman Emperor was reduced to a shadow; religious toleration was won by the Calvinists; and the independence of the Netherlands was recognized. War left German lands in a state of chaos for almost a generation. Slow recovery of the empire: imperial forces drove Turks from Hungary, 1682-1699, but not before the Turks' last siege of Vienna, 1683.

Death of the last male heir of the Hapsburg line (Charles VI, 1711-1740), who had tried to secure the rights of his daughter, Maria Theresa (1740-1780), to the Austrian throne by means of the Pragmatic Sanction, led to the War of the Austrian Succession, 1740-1748.

"Diplomatic revolution" ended the long rivalry between France and Austria and brought them into alliance against Prussia and England during the Seven Years' War, 1756-1763.

Reign of Joseph II (1765-1790) marked the era of "enlightened despotism" in Austria.

5. Holland and Sweden

A. HOLLAND. War of Dutch Independence (two phases: 1568-1609 and 1621-1648) resulted in recognition of Holland's independence at Peace of Westphalia, 1648: duke of Alva sent by Spain to suppress Dutch revolt, 1567; declaration of Dutch independence, 1581; death of William the Silent (prince of Orange), 1584; beginning of Dutch mercantile expansion and overseas settlement, *c.* 1595; twelve years' truce between Dutch and Spaniards, 1609-1621; renewal of hostilities, 1621-1648, ended in formal recognition of Dutch freedom.

B. SWEDEN. Gustavus I (Vasa) led successful rebellion against Denmark, 1520, and became king, 1523-1560; beginning of Swedish expansion into Baltic region. Sweden accepted Lutheranism, 1527. Eric XIV, 1560-1568, continued expansion of Swedish power in Baltic area. Gustavus Adolphus, 1611-1632, made Sweden the leading Baltic power; intervened successfully in Thirty Years' War (see Holy Roman Empire above). Reign of Charles XII, 1697-1718, marked the decline of Swed-

Denmark, Spain, Sweden (under its great king, Gustavus Adolphus), and France, had all taken part on one or the other side in the conflict. The war had three significant results in that at its conclusion (Peace of Westphalia, 1648), the hope of uniting all German-speaking lands under a single ruler was virtually ended until the 19th century, Spain was further weakened as a major European power, and France had emerged as the strongest continental state.

5. Holland and Sweden

The 17th century also saw the rise of two lesser states, Holland and Sweden, to brief periods of greatness. Holland, following a long struggle against Spain for her independence, became, after 1600, one of the leading colonial powers of Europe. By developing her seapower and commercial skills, this small country was able to play the role of a great state until the beginning of the 17th century, despite a relatively small population and a scarcity of natural resources. Sweden, on the other hand, while even poorer in resources and population, had the advantage of able leadership and excellent military organization which made it possible for the Swedes to dominate the Baltic regions and parts of northern Europe throughout the 17th century. With the rise of Russia after 1700, Sweden's position rapidly declined to that of a lesser European state.

ish power: Swedes defeated by Russians at Poltava, 1709; treaty of Nystadt, 1721, ended Sweden's dominance of the Baltic.

Hostilities with Russia renewed by Sweden in an effort to regain lost territories, 1741-43. By terms of the Treaty of Abö (1743) Sweden was forced to cede Finland to the Russians. Third Russian war, 1788-90, achieved initial successes; Swedes finally forced to conclude the Treaty of Wereloe which left Russia in possession of Finland and Karelia.

B. The Shift to Eastern Europe: Prussia and Russia

1. Prussia (Brandenburg)

Union of Prussia and the electorate of Brandenburg by inheritance, 1618. Reign of Frederick William the Great Elector, 1640-1688, saw the building of a strong army and a centralized government. Frederick III, elector of Brandenburg, assumed title of "King in Prussia," 1701. Frederick William I (1713-1740) created powerful Prussian army. Frederick II (the Great), 1740-1786, conquered Silesia in the War of the Austrian Succession, 1740-1748, and in alliance with England against Austria, France, and Russia successfully fought to keep it during the Seven Years' War, 1756-1763. Prussia remained one of the leading military powers of Europe until the Napoleonic era.

Treaty of Hubertusburg, 1763, guaranteed Prussia's retention of the conquered territory of Silesia. Series of domestic measures undertaken by Frederick II intended to restore Prussia after the war: remission of provincial taxes; establishment of central bank at Berlin (1765); major drainage projects undertaken. For all of these efforts, Prussia remained a not very happy model of 18th-century autocracy.

B. The Shift to Eastern Europe: Prussia and Russia

Until the end of the 17th century the focus of European events was upon the long-established states and kingdoms of western Europe. After 1700 this focus was broadened to include two new states, Prussia and Russia, whose emergence as major powers was to alter permanently the old system of international relationships in Europe. Both of these new monarchies came into existence at a time when absolutism was at its height in the West and were, therefore, able to incorporate into their system of government all the institutions and practices of the new absolutism without at the same time accepting the long-established forms of law and the customary sanctions which tended to limit the powers of western absolute monarchs. As a consequence, the sovereigns of Prussia and Russia were able to construct state systems which were far more efficient in the exercise of power, far more authoritarian, and, in some ways, far more ruthless than any existing in western Europe.

1. Prussia

With small exaggeration, it is possible to say that the kingdom of Prussia was created by a continuous and deliberate act of will on the part of an able line of north German princes whose reigns extended over a period of about 150 years (1640-1786). The territory from which these Hohenzollern rulers first began to expand their power consisted of the old border or march (mark) lands of Brandenburg in north central Germany, an area neither particularly fertile nor unusually endowed with natural resources. By clever manipulation and remarkable foresight, the rulers of Brandenburg (known as "electoral princes" in the 17th century and as "kings in Prussia" after 1701) were able to outmaneuver their neighbors diplomatically and to build up their civil service and army with such effect that by the opening of the 18th century their small state of Prussia had expanded into a formidable European power. With the accession of Frederick the Great (1740-1786), the new kingdom possessed a leader of genius and daring who led his country in successful wars with its far more powerful neighbors and, at one period during the Seven Years' War (1756-1763), actually kept at bay a powerful alliance of Austria, France, and Russia. The great effort required for so small a country to maintain itself as a major power forced the Prussian state to subordinate other forms of social activity to the interests of the military

2. Russia

Reign of Ivan III (the Great), 1462-1505, first Russian national ruler. Ivan IV (1533-1584) formally assumed title of tsar (czar, caesar) and thus laid claim to the pretensions of the Byzantine emperors. Russian patriarchate separate from that of Constantinople established, 1589.

Civil war ("time of troubles") resulted in the calling of the Romanov dynasty to the Russian throne, 1613.

Peter I (the Great), 1689-1725, undertook to "westernize" Russia and to transform it into a significant European power. His aims: (1) to give Russia an outlet to the sea; (2) to make the country strong militarily and economically by introducing West European skills; and (3) to increase the central authority of the state over church and nobles. In the Great Northern War, 1700-21, Peter broke Sweden's power in the north; though first defeated by Charles XII at Narva, 1700, Peter later won a decisive victory over the Swedes at Poltava, 1709. Peter's internal reforms: nobility made to serve the state; industry and trade encouraged; government of the Orthodox Church brought under control of the state. Treaty of Nystadt, 1721, marked Russia's emergence as the leading northern power. Russia emerged as a major European military power by participating in the Seven Years' War, 1756-63, in alliance with Austria and France against Frederick the Great. First Russian university founded in Moscow, 1755. Reign of Catherine the Great, 1762-96, saw an extension of Peter the Great's work of reform; Russian expansion in Turkey and Siberia began; ancient kingdom of Poland partitioned among Russia, Austria, and Prussia in 1772, 1793, and 1795.

C. The World of 18th-Century Europe

Overseas expansion and settlement during the seventeenth century.

The seventeenth century witnessed a less spectacular

establishment and led to the founding of a military caste and a tradition as harsh and demanding in its way as that of Sparta in the ancient world.

2. Russia

Of equal significance to western civilization was the emergence of Russia as a European power during the same period. For centuries the Slavic peoples of the great east European plain had been isolated from the mainstream of west European development. During the early middle ages Latin Christian missionaries had converted the Poles (*c.* 963) and brought the medieval kingdom of Poland into western Christendom, while, at about the same time, German colonists, pushing eastward across the Elbe and Oder rivers, had conquered and Christianized other groups of Slavs. Both movements had stopped short of the area now known as Russia which, as a consequence, came under influences and developed a society and customs somewhat different from those of the west European community of states. There the missionary efforts of the Greek Orthodox Church brought Russian lands within the Greek Christian orbit; then a period of Tartar rule, beginning in the 13th century, kept the peoples of the area in isolation from the West. Not until the 15th century did the modern state begin to expand outward from the principality of Muscovy (Moscow). As it grew, its rulers began to think of themselves as the Caesars (czars or tsars) of the "third Rome" and took on the style and manner of Byzantine autocrats, while their power was greatly enhanced by the unsettled conditions of the Russian frontiers. By the 17th century the Russian state was pressing hard against the older Slavic kingdoms of Poland and Lithuania as it gradually moved its borders westward.

At this juncture there came to the Russian throne the famous "westernizing" Tsar Peter the Great (1689-1725), who deliberately initiated a policy intended to bring Russia up to the western level of military and economic strength. With ruthless energy he made his country a European power for the first time in its history. Though it was for long inferior to the rest of Europe in its economic and technical development, the appearance of such a vast sprawling state with its expansionist tendencies was to change the European balance of power permanently.

C. The World of 18th-Century Europe

By the opening of 18th century, a significant change had taken place in the relations of western Europe with the rest of the world. While Europe's wars were still fought over European objectives—namely, terbut more consistent expansion of European holdings overseas. If there were few major discoveries, colonization and development went on apace so that by the end of the century that worldwide commercial network created by the European imperial system had virtually come into being. In general, European colonization tended to follow three patterns: (1) in regions like Latin America a resident aristocracy of Spaniards and Portuguese ruled a large and long-settled but relatively primitive population who worked for the ruling Europeans as a labor force; to some extent the Europeans intermarried with the native population; (2) elsewhere, in North America for example, where the native population was too sparse to furnish an adequate labor force, Europeans pushed the natives aside and established European communities whose inhabitants lived by their own labors and in so doing made use of European skills and techniques; (3) in most parts of Africa and Asia the Europeans did not settle in great numbers but sought only to establish trading stations and to develop commercial monopolies.

D. The 18th-Century Struggle for Overseas Empire

In the Peace of Utrecht (1713; War of the Spanish Succession) Britain gained from France: Acadia, Hudson's Bay, Newfoundland, and St. Kitts; from Spain, Gibraltar and the right to trade with Spanish colonies for 30 years (the *Asiento*).

The Treaty of Aix-la-Chapelle (1748; War of the Austrian Succession) provided for the mutual restoration of colonial conquests.

In the Treaty of Paris (1763; Seven Years' War) Britain gained from France: Canada and Cape Breton Island, Grenada in the West Indies, and French possessions on the Senegal in Africa; from Spain, Florida. Britain restored Goree in Africa ritorial rivalries, dynastic ambitions, and power alignments—a new and important element began to play an often decisive part in the diplomatic and military strategy of European states. Heretofore, struggles over colonies or commercial concessions in other parts of the world had been localized affairs which did not always affect the welfare or the position of a particular state in international politics. After 1700, however, victory or defeat in remote areas like India or North America could often determine the outcome of a European war.

The reason for this change is not far to seek. A significant part of Europe's economic well-being now depended upon overseas connections. Great amounts of capital and large numbers of Europeans had migrated to lands outside Europe. Indirectly, of course, the economic power of the new relationship had been making itself felt in Europe for generations. Since the 16th century the gold and silver brought to Spain from the new world had been pumped, in the regular course of commercial exchange, into the European economic system. As a result, the decline in the purchasing power of money, which had been observable in European life from the 15th century onward, became more marked; indeed, it was a "price revolution" which enormously increased the cost of living. The effects of this sudden increase were far-reaching and contributed to the economic hardship not only of individuals but even of governments. The financial difficulties of many European monarchs during the 16th and 17th centuries, which in turn caused political tensions and upheavals, are indirectly traceable to this economic revolution. In this sense, the European economy was already global, and Europe itself was the center of a complex network of relationships reaching outward to all parts of the earth.

D.   The 18th-Century Struggle for Overseas Empire

Two nations, England and France, were more directly involved in and affected by this transformation during the 18th century than any others. Holland and Spain both had passed the zenith of their power, and no other continental states were in a position to challenge Anglo-French hegemony outside Europe. As a consequence, these two were the major antagonists in a long series of intermittent struggles for empire which lasted for almost a century and terminated on the eve of the French Revolution. In each of these conflicts, beginning with the War of the Spanish Succession (1702-1713), through the War of the Austrian Succession (1740-1748), the Seven Years' War (1756-1763), and ending with the War of the American Revolution (1778-1783), England was and Pondichery and Chandernagor in India to France; Cuba was returned by Britain to Spain. This treaty marked the height of Britain's colonial power in the 18th century.

In the Treaty of Paris (1783; War of the American Revolution) Britain granted independence to American colonies, Tobago and Senegal to France, Minorca and Florida to Spain. This was the only colonial war of the century in which Britain lost more than she gained.

almost regularly victorious. Only in the War of the American Revolution did she suffer any reversal. It was during this century that England acquired vast territories which historians have come to call the First British Empire, since a great deal of it, including her colonies in North America, was lost in 1783. She did, however, come into possession of Canada and retain it, and she cemented her hold upon large parts of the subcontinent of India.

CHAPTER 9

The Scientific Revolution
and the Age of the Enlightenment

THE ESSENTIAL MOVEMENT

During few periods of his history has western man ever really possessed the confidence to believe that by his reasoning alone he could fathom all the questions about himself and his existence. For the greater part of his historic life man has sensed something unknown or mysterious that lies just beyond his powers of rational explanation. Traditionally, he has assigned that unknown to the sphere of religious faith, confessing that the universe in all of its mystery is truly explicable only in terms of the divine. On a few historic occasions, however, the elation of a great and significant intellectual discovery, which seems to push the boundaries of his understanding deep into the unknown, has raised his confidence in his own powers to a point where he believes himself capable, after all, of finally answering the questions that have puzzled him since the beginning of time. One period when men came close to achieving this confidence was during the age of Greek intellectual greatness in the 5th and 4th centuries B.C. Another began with the opening of the 18th century, reached its zenith a few decades later, and carried over, at least in the sphere of scientific thought, into the 19th and 20th centuries. Much of this confidence remains with us, though doubting voices have been raised in our own time to question, once again, the possibility of man's ultimately knowing all that there is to know about himself and his universe.

EVENTS AND DEFINITIONS

A. The Scientific Revolution

Many of the earliest and most significant scientific discoveries of the early modern period were made in the field of
astronomy. Some of the more important of these were: (1)
the formulation of the heliocentric (sun-centered) theory of
the solar system by Copernicus (1473-1543) whose *On the
Revolution of Celestial Bodies* transformed the bases of scientific thought; (2) Johannes Kepler (1571-1630) formulated his
three laws of planetary motion; (3) Galileo Galilei (1564-1642)
perfected telescope (1609) which proved the Copernican theory; Galileo also formulated the laws of "local motion" (mechanics); (4) Isaac Newton (1642-1727) published his conclusions on the laws of celestial mechanics (theory of gravitation)
in *Principia mathematica* (1687); Pierre Simon de Laplace
(1749-1827) completed and developed the Newtonian astronomy in his *Système du Monde* (1796).

Mathematics and Natural Philosophy: Francis Bacon
(1561-1626) set forth his inductive method and prepared the
way for modern experimental method in his *Novum Organ-
um*; René Descartes (1596-1650) wrote *Discourse on Method*
and first applied algebraic method to geometry; Blaise Pascal
(1632-1662) discovered mathematical theory of probability;
Newton and G. W. Leibniz (1646-1716), the German philosopher, independently discovered the Calculus; Joseph Lagrange
(1736-1813) created the calculus of variations and systema-
tized differential equations.

Medicine, Biology, and Chemistry: Theophrastus von
Hohenheim (Paracelsus), c. 1490-1541, broke with the medical tradition of Galen and used chemical drugs in medical
practice; Andreas Vesalius, 1515-1564, published his great
work on anatomy, *Fabrica Humani Corporis* in 1543; William
Harvey, 1578-1657, formulated a general theory of blood circulation in his *On the Motion of the Heart* (1628); Anton van
Leeuwenhoek, 1632-1723, Dutch microscopist, did not invent
the microscope but he did perfect the technique of micro-
scopic observation in scientific experiments; John Ray, 1627-
1705, laid the foundations of modern descriptive and system-
atic biology; Carl Linnaeus (von Linne), 1707-1778, evolved
the first successful system of biological classification (1735);
Georges Cuvier, 1769-1832, founded the modern science of

A. The Scientific Revolution

What gave the 18th century its confidence in the power of man's reason to reduce the unknown was a revolution in thought which had occurred in the century preceding. The 17th century was a "century of genius" in the words of a great modern scientific philosopher, a time when a whole galaxy of outstanding figures suddenly appeared on the intellectual horizon of Europe. Why men like Galileo, Descartes, Newton, or Leibniz should have been born within the brief span of a single century is something no one can explain. In part, their achievements in what we now call the field of science may have been the result of accident. More probably they were the result of a combination of complex social factors that came together at a particular moment and produced the intellectual stimuli needed for such discoveries.

Another part of the explanation must surely lie in the fact that certain underlying ideas or assumptions, many of them reaching back to the Greeks, were shared by all those who speculated in the natural sciences. The most important of these was the assumption that the universe was an ordered and orderly system so regulated that it could be understood by those who had the knowledge, the patience, and the intelligence to do so. The assumption of order in nature was the basis of philosophy and mathematics and had, for centuries, been implicit in the belief that the universe was controlled by fixed and certain natural laws. This faith, however much it may have been modified during the period between the fall of Rome and the high middle ages, had never been entirely lost and was, as we have seen, an important part of the intellectual heritage of the medieval philosophers.

The major difficulty with this assumption that the universe was rational and orderly lay in the fact that much of what men were able to observe empirically, i.e., through their senses, did not always seem to square with the harmony expressed in mathematics and natural law. Fortunately for modern science, thinkers of the later middle ages and the Renaissance were not daunted by this apparent contradiction, which made it seem, for example, that the sun traveled round the earth. As the science of mathematics continued to develop, men continued to make use of it to test, to probe, and to explain all the seemingly disordered phenomena of the world in which they lived. In so doing, they sometimes ran foul of the theories of Aristotle, on which a part of medieval theology was based, and thus came into conflict with ecclesiastical authority. Despite these difficulties, their own intellectual aspirations drove them to continue their efforts until a major break-through had paleontology; Johann van Helmont, c. 1580-1644, first studied chemical gases; Robert Boyle, 1627-91, sought to make clear the fundamental nature of chemical transformation in his *Sceptical Chymist* (1661); Joseph Priestley, 1733-1804, isolated oxygen; Antoine Lavoisier, 1743-94, proved that while matter may alter its state as a result of chemical reactions it does not alter its amount.

Scientific Academies: one of the ways in which scientific knowledge was accumulated and spread was through the organization of learned bodies or academies. Among the more famous of these were: Accademia Secretorum Naturae (Naples), 1560; Accademia dei Lincei, of which Galileo was a member (Rome), 1603-30; Royal Society of London, 1662; Académie des Sciences (Paris), 1666.

B. The Enlightenment

The Newtonian discoveries appeared to reinforce a method of inquiry first put forward by Descartes (1596-1650) that seemed to promise great possibilities for the study of man and human society. By searching every field of knowledge for basic axioms whose truth could not be doubted when subjected to the most searching analyses, men might hope to erect a "social science" as accurate and valid as the physical sciences. John Locke (1632-1704), English philosopher and political theorist, provided the basis for the later philosophies of the Enlightenment in his *Essay Concerning Human Understanding* been achieved in the field of astronomy, where many of the great advances in early modern science were made. The man responsible for this discovery was Nicholas Copernicus (1473-1543), who found that by assuming the sun rather than the earth as the center of the system of planets he could explain the movements of the sun, moon, stars, earth, and planets much more clearly and in simpler mathematical terms. It is important to remember here that Copernicus did not have empirical evidence for the heliocentric theory (sun-centered) when he offered it in place of the geocentric theory (earth-centered). For the evidence of the senses indicated to him, as it had to men for centuries, that the sun went around the earth. Copernicus proposed the new hypothesis out of a belief that nature was orderly and that this orderliness was compatible with the simpler mathematical expression that the new theory permitted.

With this discovery, the whole science of mathematics, and with it astronomy, underwent a revolution that had far-reaching effects. Within a hundred and fifty years the search for ever more precise mathematical expressions of natural law had led to the formulation of the laws of mechanics by Galileo and finally to the crowning achievement of the whole scientific revolution, the famous hypothesis of Sir Isaac Newton by which the relations of all bodies in the universe were explained according to three basic laws. The appearance of Newton's *Principles of Mathematics* in 1687 was the signal for a major change in the intellectual climate of western civilization, for by that time each of the great discoveries had been seemingly verified beyond question with the invention of new measuring devices and new methods of observation. The result seemed to foretell a marvelous future for the human race which, at last, appeared to possess a means of plumbing all knowledge.

B. The Enlightenment: the Intellectual Impact of the Scientific Revolution

Newton's discoveries had the effect of transforming the thinking of large numbers of Europeans. The new thinking exalted every form of scientific knowledge. Science accordingly has grown in prestige until it has come to be looked upon by many persons in the western world as the most important of all intellectual activities. But Newton's discoveries had an immediate effect which has not proved wholly good, since they convinced many persons that all the complexities of the universe, including the diverse and seemingly unpredictable vagaries of human relations, could in the same way be reduced to relatively simple mechanical laws akin to those of the physical sciences. Newton, it seemed to

(1690). Locke declared that he would "inquire into the original, certainty, and extent of human knowledge." His purpose, though seemingly at odds with the methods of Descartes, was really to preserve Cartesian rationalism. Locke believed that all knowledge derived from the senses, that the mind of man was a blank slate or *tabula rasa* which is gradually filled with sensory information drawn from experience. In short, Locke, though his writings later were seen to have opened the way for an empirical attack on rationalism, really wanted a "middle way" which would comprehend both rationalism and empiricism. In the two generations after Locke his empirical suggestions were carried to a conclusion by two other British "empirical" philosophers: (1) Bishop George Berkeley, 1685-1753, taught in his *Theory of Vision* (1709) that "all that we see is our sensation" and in his *Principles of Human Knowledge*, 1710, that "all that exists is our knowledge." Matter, as Berkeley saw it, had no existence independent of human perception. (2) David Hume, 1711-1776, carried empiricism to its extreme conclusion in his *Treatise on Human Nature* (1739) and thus prepared the way for the philosophical reconstruction of Immanuel Kant and the Romantic School of philosophers.

1. Religion

Growth of deism or "natural religion":
Voltaire (1694-1778) spread the ideas of the English deists in his *Letters on the English* (1734) and his *Elements of the Philosophy of Newton* (1738).

David Hume (1711-1776), the Scottish philosopher, expressed religious skepticism in his *Dialogues Concerning Natural Religion* (1779).

The leading materialist (atheist) work was Baron Holbach's *System of Nature* (1770), which described the universe as a place where no divine authority exists.

Deism, which was most widely accepted in England, was represented by the following:

Anthony Collins, 1676-1729, first put forward the Deist position in his *Discourse on Free Thinking* (1713).

Matthew Tindal, 1653-1733, author of the most comprehensive treatise on Deism, *Christianity as Old as the Creation* many in the 18th century, had provided the key that would unlock all the mysteries of the universe. Man's task was simply to determine what the underlying laws of nature were and, by use of his reason, adjust to them so that he could live in harmony with his world. The first half of the 18th century thus became a confident Age of Reason in which it was assumed that man was an "enlightened" creature (hence the term "Enlightenment" used to describe the period) whose power to perfect himself was unlimited. No longer were men to be thought of as inherently wicked beings, imperfect and infected with original sin—men, whether they were good or evil, were products of the environment in which they lived. That men were evil, if they were, was the result of evils in their surroundings, of the bad institutions or wicked superstitions inherited from their unenlightened forebears. What man needed above all to progress (and the word "progress" was one of the great watchwords of the Enlightenment) was freedom to develop his powers of reason and to reform the evils in the world about him so that as he improved materially he would also improve morally. He had to have liberty to express himself freely, to worship as he wished, and to choose those things his reason told him were good. As a consequence, the great writers of the Enlightenment, particularly in France, were not only strong social critics but also defenders of a philosophy of "enlightened individualism."

The influence of these basic ideas reached out to touch every kind of thought. Let us now look at some of the most important of their effects.

1. Religion

In the area of religious belief the most important single effect stemming from the Scientific Revolution and the Enlightenment was a weakening of faith among the intellectual classes of Europe. It had not been the intention of many of the great scientific thinkers of the 17th century to destroy Christian theology or to weaken the basis of belief. Many of them—Newton, for example—were profoundly religious men. Inevitably, however, some of the things they said, simply because their statements seemed to be at variance with teachings long accepted as orthodox, created serious tensions between themselves and churchmen of all denominations. A great part of the difficulty arose from the fact that by stressing the importance, the permanence, and the unchanging nature of the physical laws that controlled the universe, the scientific thinkers of the period appeared to imply that God was only a sort of watchmaker who, having made the universe and set it in motion, then left it to its own devices. Such an implication challenged the stories of divine intervention in human affairs as related by scripture and the Christian tradi-

(1730), sometimes called the "Bible of Deism."

William Wollaston, 1659-1724, argued in favor of the adequacy of "a religion of reason" to serve men's needs in his *The Religion of Nature Delineated* (1722).

As the century advanced, however, there was a strong reaction among many religious groups to both Deism and rationalism. Among the more important of these groups were: John Wesley, 1703-91, and his followers, later (1784) known as Methodists, who preached salvation through faith in Christ alone; Moravian Brethren in Germany who reorganized them-selves in 1732; Israel B. Eliezer (Baal-Schem-Tov), 1700-60, founder of the devout pietistic Jewish group known as the Hasidim.

2. Political Theory

Just as John Locke was the leading proponent of the philosophy of the Enlightenment, so was he also in large meas-ure the founder of its political theory. That is not to say that everyone in the 18th century accepted what Locke had to say without question. Nevertheless, Locke's *Two Treatises of Gov-ernment* (1690), which were actually written to justify the English Revolution of 1688, came to be widely accepted by the European literate community during the hundred years after the *Treatises* appeared. In brief, Locke argued that gov-ernment (including even kings) was responsible to the gov-erned as a consequence of a mythical contract entered into when society was first formed. If the contract was broken by the ruler, then the community had the right to rebel. The idea was based upon a questionable historical hypothesis but, none-theless, had a wide influence on the thought of 18th-century Europe. The notion of limited power was carried over into French thought by Montesquieu (1689-1755) in his *Spirit of Laws*, 1748. C. A. Helvetius (1715-1771) sought to give po-litical theory a "scientific" basis by arguing that the only rational standard of conduct was one based upon the "greatest good for the greatest number;" he published *De l'esprit (Of the Spirit)* in 1758. J. J. Rousseau (1712-1778) in his *Social Contract*, 1762, put forward the idea that society as a whole is possessed of a "general will" which directs the affairs of government. Publication of the *Encyclopedia* under the edition—miracles became impossible because they were in violation of an inviolable natural law. Even more disturbing: such a mechanistic implication made men wonder about the accuracy of scripture itself. Impelled by doubts, many scholars turned to re-examine the Bible in a new critical light, and their findings inevitably raised new questions. From this dilemma of reason and faith men found various escapes. Some denied its existence and reaffirmed their traditional beliefs. Others, most notably the school of philosopher-theologians known as the Deists, sought a form of compromise in which God was deemed not a personal deity in the Christian sense but a remote, impersonal "Supreme Being." A few went the whole way to atheism and argued that the universe, which seemed on the basis of physical law to have existed through all eternity, had no creator but was a kind of timeless machine existing without a beginning or an end.

2. Political Theory

The political theory of the Enlightenment derived from the fundamental belief that man is a creature of his environment who needs only to improve his surroundings in order to progress toward earthly perfection. In those parts of Europe, England for example, where the state and society seemed conducive to a certain amount of individual freedom and where the power of rational choice appeared not to be markedly restricted by social traditions and political institutions, the ideals and aspirations of the Enlightenment strengthened the social order. In France, on the other hand, because of growing discontent with inequities in taxation, bureaucratic inefficiency, and the entrenched position of the nobility, the ideas of the Enlightenment took on a revolutionary cast. Furthermore, the arguments of the French *philosophes* (philosophers) were reinforced in popular thinking by the successive military defeats sustained by France at the hands of England during the first half of the 18th century. As a consequence of these, Frenchmen inevitably asked what it was that gave England her advantage and concluded that it lay in the superiority of England's enlightened institutions and traditions. Leading thinkers like Voltaire and Montesquieu became ardent admirers of all things English, which they held up to Frenchmen as enlightened models. From England, too, were imported certain social and political theories originally developed by Thomas Hobbes (1588-1679) and John Locke (1632-1704) which, in French hands, were to become dangerous intellectual weapons.

Basically, however, the political theory of the Enlightenment, while it varied from individual to individual, held that as a rational being man torship of Denis Diderot (1713-1784), a work which summarized the ideals of the Enlightenment, 1751-1765. Marquis de Condorcet (1743-1794) best expressed the Enlightenment's faith in human progress in his *Progress of the Human Spirit*, 1794.

3. Economic Theory

The belief that there were laws governing economic activity was first given coherent form in the writings of the French physiocrats whose most important writer, Dr. Francis Quesnay (1694-1774), published influential articles in the *Encyclopedia*, 1756-1757, and his major work, *Tableau économique*, in 1756. The essence of physiocratic doctrine was a belief in the "natural order" of economic activity. Quesnay and his followers argued that wealth was not gold and silver but sprang from production and flowed through the nation to replenish the whole of society. The difficulty with physiocracy, however, was that its adherents insisted that agriculture alone produced wealth and that merchants and manufacturers only manipulated it for their own ends. Under physiocratic influences A. R. J. Turgot (1727-1781), the great French finance minister, published his *Reflections on the Formation and Distribution of Wealth*, 1766. Adam Smith, 1723-1790, after a visit to France in 1764-66 incorporated a number of physiocratic ideas into his *Wealth of Nations*, 1776. Smith's great work was not just simply a statement of *laissez-faire* principles. He was concerned to show what the mechanism was by which society functions. In explanation he formulated the laws of the market. What he strove to demonstrate was the way in which all men by pursuing their own interests would seek, as if led by an "invisible hand," the end "which is most agreeable to the interest of the whole society." Thomas Malthus (1766-1834) in his *Essay on the Principle of Population*, 1798, challenged the optimism of the 18th century by arguing that population always tends to far outstrip the means of subsistence.

had the right to create his own political institutions if those already in existence did not conform to the standards of his reason. This view did not necessarily lead to democracy, since, in the opinion of many *philosophes*, not all men had reached the level of rationality needed to make democracy work. It did imply, however—though many thinkers preferred to trust an enlightened monarch—that all those possessed of reasoning power, knowledge, and education could or should have some part in governing themselves. This belief was capable of ultimate enormous expansion and could lead to revolutionary conclusions.

3. Economic Theory

Just as the physical universe had its laws, so, too, it was assumed during the Enlightenment that human social and economic relationships were also governed by laws which it was the duty of the rational man to seek out and understand. Under the influence of this kind of thinking a great deal of new attention was devoted to understanding man's relations with his material environment and his fellow humans. To this end, society was studied as never before, and, for the first time, a serious attempt was made to create what we now call the "social sciences."

The most popular and famous of these many attempts was the work of Adam Smith, whose *Wealth of Nations*, published in 1776 was to become the Bible of the new social science of "political economy" (later to be known as "economics"). Smith was not merely a theorist of the Enlightenment, however. He was also an antagonist of certain economic theories and practices, like the restrictive system of mercantilsm, which he felt were dangerously limiting the economic growth of European society. The theory of mercantilism, whose greatest exponent had been the French finance minister Colbert (1619-1683), was derived from the belief that all trade and manufacturing had to be strictly controlled in the interests of the state. Commercial activity under mercantilism was the analogue of warfare, in which a nation strove to amass wealth by accumulating bullion (gold and silver), or by exporting goods of greater money value than it imported from its neighbors. Against this view (though he did feel that the state had the right to impose some restrictions when national interests were at stake), Smith argued that the economic world was governed by a body of laws all its own which had nothing to do with politics or the policies of states. Economic systems were controlled by natural laws which could not be flouted at the whim of human beings. Men should be left free to follow their own enlightened self-interest in economic matters and, in so doing would be acting in harmony with those laws. To facilitate this freedom, every form of restriction, tariff, or other

4. Enlightened Despotism

Frederick the Great of Prussia (1740-1786) described himself as "the first servant of the state"; worked to improve the economic conditions of Prussia; friendly with Voltaire and other philosophers of the Enlightenment; spoke French in preference to German and interested himself in philosophy and the arts.

Catherine the Great of Russia (1762-1796): patronized the French *philosophes;* codified Russian laws; interested herself in the philosophy of the Enlightenment.

Joseph II of Austria (1765-1790): one of the few rulers who really believed in enlightened despotism; tried to institute popular education; reformed the legal code; promoted religious toleration even in the face of strong opposition from his own subjects.

barrier to unfettered trade should be abolished, and men should be let alone *(laissez-faire)* to engage in economic activity. The purpose of government was to provide social stability, security of life and property, and enforcement of contracts. If it did these things and nothing more, men, left to themselves to seek their own rational economic ends, would also ultimately serve the welfare of society as a whole.

4. Enlightened Despotism: the Political Effect of the Enlightenment

With the wide dissemination of the teachings of the Enlightenment, 18th-century Europe witnessed the rise of a new phenomenon known as "enlightened despotism." To a large extent, the system of enlightened despotism was only an extension of the older forms of absolute monarchy; but it was absolute monarchy with a difference. By the middle of the 18th century it was no longer fashionable, even among kings, to insist that their rule was justified solely by inheritance or divine right. The sovereign, following the example of the kings of Prussia, was the "first servant of the state" and was obligated to provide for the general welfare of his people by giving them efficient government, reforms when needed, and equal justice. In short, the enlightened despot, by endeavoring to rule according to the dictates of reason, justified his authority on the purely secular grounds of usefulness. Furthermore, under the influence of the prevailing ideas, he often promoted reforms which were opposed by large numbers of his subjects. For this reason, the rule of the enlightened despot might be called paternal in the sense that change was accomplished for the good of the people whether they liked it or not. But the enlightened despots were not necessarily motivated by the prevailing ideas. Many of their reforms were carried out as a means of organizing the resources of their kingdoms for greater efficiency in waging war against their neighbors and not with the welfare of their subjects in mind.

CHAPTER 10

The Western World in 1700: A Summary and Conclusion

THE ESSENTIAL MOVEMENT

By the year 1700, western civilization had reached a point in its historic development where it was possible to forecast the pattern of later events. Political events were in train that did not culminate until the end of the century, and these we have considered in a preceding chapter. Movements in the fields of science and philosophy were also in train. Almost all of the distinctive qualities that were to give wealth and power to the West during the next 250 years had already begun to evolve out of the complex of European life. Europeans had conquered and settled vast areas beyond the seas. Scientific ideas, technological skills, and productive techniques, though they were to bring about an "industrial revolution" in the century after 1700, had, even by that date, advanced to a stage where the West for the first time in its history produced more goods and wealth than any other area on earth. The European mind, strongly influenced by the ideas of the Scientific Revolution of the 17th century, was already confidently conscious of the possibility that all the Big Questions about man and the universe might at last be answered. In the sphere of political life the state had reached a point in its evolution where more was expected of it than ever before: in response to the expectation it had expanded both its authority and bureaucracy but had been less successful in expanding its revenues. For a long time, too, the state had confronted a growing complexity in its relations with those whom it ruled, and some European countries had already passed through the turmoil of civil war and revolution which was symptomatic of this inherent difficulty.

In the light of these developments let us now turn our attention, once again, to the four major themes discussed in the introduction to this volume and see just how each of them had evolved up to the opening of the 18th century.

1. Human Control over the World of Nature (the Material Environment)

At the beginning of the 18th century western man had come a long way in his struggle to mitigate the adverse influences of his environment. Though he had not yet discovered new sources of energy to supplant those usually found in nature—i.e., wind, water, and human or animal power—and though it may be doubted that any of his inventions or discoveries for some thousands of years had been as fundamentally significant as those made during the Neolithic Revolution, yet, despite reverses and periods when his cultural achievements fell below those of preceding generations, he had refined the techniques by which he won his subsistence and added to the details of his varied knowledge in many ways.

In one important respect, however, his achievements had not followed a path of continuous progress. With the collapse of Rome and the disintegration of a unified Mediterranean civilization the historic continuity of human knowledge, though not entirely broken, was very much attenuated in many regions that had been part of the Roman Empire (and particularly in those inhabited by the Germanic peoples). For some centuries there was no longer an extensive or consistent interchange or expansion of ideas and techniques throughout the region we now know as Europe; and for that reason the years between about 500 and 1000 A.D. must be thought of, to some extent, as "dark ages." Yet we should bear in mind that learning, even in the classic sense, was never entirely lost and that there were forces at work during those centuries which deny the stereotyped description of those historians who like to think of the period as one of unrelieved ignorance.

Here and there in isolated places significant technological advances were made; but knowledge of them spread slowly, and frequently skills were lost from one generation to another because those who knew of them were limited in number or lived in places remote from the areas of greatest population. What this era lacked, perhaps more than anything else, was institutional continuity of the kind that preserves and conveys knowledge from one generation to the next. The great universities of later medieval Europe did not yet exist, and the church had not yet become the highly rationalized and cohesive international organization that it would be in the high middle ages. For while it is true that the Latin church through its monastic centers helped to keep "the lamp of learning alight," it had not regained the traditions of the Roman administrative system, the efficiency, or the centralized authority which had disappeared with the disintegration of the western empire.

Whatever the reason, since the causes are not yet entirely clear to us, there began some time toward the end of the 10th or beginning of the 11th century a series of movements which reinvigorated the life of the West and ushered in another period of expansion. Population growth may have played a part in it, but this we cannot know with certainty because we lack statistics. Furthermore, the mere growth of human numbers has never been a guarantee of resultant intellectual or technical expansion but in many societies has forced down living standards and caused intellectual stagnation. Undoubtedly, the Cluniac and later Gregorian reforms (so called after Pope Gregory VII) played a part in this change by revitalizing that greatest of medieval institutions, the church, which in turn spread the new leaven through medieval society. This effect may best be seen in the founding of new monastic orders and the growth of universities. As important as any of these was an economic and technological expansion marked, on the one hand, by the founding of new cities and the growth of old ones and, on the other, by an apparent increase in agricultural and other productivity. In this area, too, we are at loss to explain all the reasons for sudden vitality. It may be that the 11th century was simply a time when a great many developments reaching far back into the western past and not easily identified by historians began to have a cumulative effect. Some historians now believe that the most important cause of this great economic change was the growth of the early feudal state which, though relatively weak and ineffective in many ways, provided the degree of security and political stability needed to stimulate economic activity.

Still we must not exaggerate the effects of this expansion by assuming that it led at once to a broad extension of human control over the material environment. Western technology, until about the 15th century, lagged behind that of some Middle Eastern and oriental societies; and western man, like everyone else, could and did suffer horribly from natural catastrophes over which he had little or no control and whose consequences often altered his way of life in curiously unpredictable ways.

Year in and year out, with fearsome regularity, he was visited by plagues and pests. Men sometimes died in such numbers—as in the Black Death of 1348-1349—that the very structure of society was altered and the course of human history undoubtedly changed. Famines were a common part of the human lot, and even the richest societies were seldom far removed from the danger of harvest failure and the horrors of mass starvation. In most European cities such elemental methods of disease prevention as drainage, sewerage, and pure water supply, which had been known to the ancients, were not used extensively until well along in the 18th and 19th centuries.

Nevertheless, the upward curve of scientific and technological achievement during the years between 1000 and 1700 was impressive. New methods of navigation and ship construction made possible longer and safer voyages. The development of military technology, while it enabled Europeans to kill one another in larger numbers, also put an end to the danger, ever present until the end of the middle ages, of outside conquest by Turks or Mongols who might have destroyed western civilization. Extensive engineering projects like the canals and dikes of Holland and the great swamp-drainage undertakings of England and France brought large areas of previously unused land under cultivation. In medicine, advances in the study of anatomy and bodily functions prepared the way for even greater successes in the future. But it was in the growth of scientific thought that the greatest potential for the future was achieved, for the 17th century was one of genius which saw the formulation of those basic scientific hypotheses which were to transform the western world during the next 250 years and make its achievements unique and greater than any in previous history. By 1700 men already believed that science might well be the means of extending the "empire of man over nature" as never before.

2. Belief in an Ordered, Purposeful Universe and Historical Progress

With scientific and technological advance, western man by 1700 had become more and more convinced that nature was governed by laws which gave order to the universe and could be made to work for man's benefit. Moreover, he was also convinced that these laws, as the discoveries of Galileo and Newton seemed to prove, could be comprehended by the human mind.

This faith in an ordered universe and the power of the mind, though very much intensified as a result of the scientific achievements of the 17th century, was no new thing in the history of western civilization. Its beginnings went back to the earliest Greek thinkers who assumed the existence of order beneath all the shifting, diverse phenomena of the everyday world. In large measure this belief was responsible for the development of Greek mathematics and the Greek attempt, best exemplified in the thought of Plato, to explain the cosmos and the relationships of the world of matter to the world of ideas. Indeed, it is the persistence of this Greek view of things, later carried over into Christian thought, that has come to be looked upon as one of the unique and significant elements in western civilization. Without such a faith western man might not have attempted to formulate the laws of modern science. Here, as in a number of other things, the West owes much to the high middle ages, the period that was for long assumed by historians to have been one of darkness and ignorance. For the medieval philosophers, though they worked within the restrictive framework of Christian belief, helped to preserve the tradition that the universe was ordered and rational by incorporating much of Greek philosophy, and particularly the writings of Aristotle, into Christian thought. In so doing they performed an important service for the West, even while they tended to hold too slavishly to the letter of Aristotle's teachings and thus, in some respects, held up the development of scientific thought during the 15th and 16th centuries: they kept alive the basic Greek way of looking at the world.

For long the significance of this service was overlooked by historians and scientists who thought of the Scientific Revolution as a complete reaction against the medieval way of looking at things. The middle ages, said they, accepted truth on the basis of revealed authority, while science is based solely upon observation and experiment; therefore, the modern scientific method as it has evolved since the 17th century is the very antithesis of medieval thought. But it is not antithesis, for the scientific method is made up of *two* important elements: one is empiricism (i.e., observation and experiment), which scientists have regarded as absolutely essential to scientific advance since the days of Galileo; the other is rationalism (i.e., the assumption that nature is governed by laws). Without this rational element which was preserved from the western past by the medieval philosophers the scientific method and the scientific way of looking at the world could not have come into being.

With the emergence of this new scientific way of thought, western man's notion of purpose in history also changed. Just as the achievements of the Scientific Revolution increased his intellectual self-confidence, so in many ways it also increased his confidence that history was a steady progression toward moral and material perfection. Like the western belief in an ordered universe, this idea was not entirely new. Both Judaism and Christianity had taught that humanity was moving toward a far-off rendezvous—a last judgment—at the end of time. But while Christians had believed in man's perfectibility, they had also been taught that such perfection was to be found only in the life hereafter.

About 1700 the essentially Christian view that humanity was moving toward the last judgment was transformed into the view that men were moving toward perfectibility in this world. The new view did not claim that each man would attain perfection in his own lifetime. Perfection was something attainable by the human race as a whole only after a long period of time had elapsed. Each generation, by adding to the sum of human knowledge, would raise mankind stage by stage toward perfection; for this was the law of progress. This new doctrine taught that progress was inevitable; never again would mankind relapse into barbarism, because human knowledge and reason were now sufficiently advanced to keep history moving in one direction, namely, forward. In this view, change was neither bad nor meaningless. On the contrary, it was always good and purposeful. It was progress, therefore good, and anything that deterred progress was bad. Thus armed with a belief that history was on his side, western man now confidently assumed that there was nothing beyond his ultimate comprehension or accomplishment.

3.   The Expansion of Europe

At the end of the 17th century the process of European expansion had already reached a stage where it was no longer a development of merely European but of worldwide significance. By the year 1700, thousands of Europeans had already ceased to be inhabitants of Europe and had taken up permanent residence overseas. In some cases this residence had extended over so many generations that Europe was a remote ancestral homeland far removed from the immediate concerns and interests of many overseas colonists. As yet no area of European settlement was politically or culturally independent of Europe, but the time of political separation for some of them was not far off. Furthermore, the European economy was already tied into a large global system of economic relations upon which Europe depended for a significant part of its commerce and for some of its material resources.

This state of affairs was the result of five different but closely related developments, each of which we must now examine briefly.

a.   Growth of Population

Since most European states had no regular census-taking procedures until the 19th century, historians and demographers (population experts) have had to rely on other, somewhat indirect evidence for their estimates of population change or growth before the year 1800. The informed consensus, however, is that the population of Europe down to about 1650 was increasing but that its growth was slow in contrast to its enormous increase after that date.

Nevertheless, all our evidence indicates that most countries had much larger populations in the year 1700 than they had in the year 1000. England, for example, is estimated to have had a population of slightly more than 1 million persons near the end of the 11th century (1086). By 1700 the estimated figure had grown to about 6 million. While these absolute figures are small in modern terms, the rate of growth is fairly substantial Even more important, however, was the enormous growth which most demographers believe began about the year 1650. Since that time—and the forces of increase were obviously at work in 1700—there has taken place, quite literally, not an expansion but an explosion of Europeans. For while it is true that today the populations of Asia and parts of Africa are numerically larger than those of Europe or of areas settled by Europeans overseas, their historic rate of increase does not appear to have been nearly so high. Again, if we look at England, the most striking example of this increase, we can see how almost unbelievably high the rate of growth has been. In 1700 there were probably fewer than 10 million English-speaking persons in all the world. By 1950 that number had grown to more than 250 million.

For both the earlier and later rates of growth there have been a number of explanations. Very probably one reason why European population grew even before 1650 was an increase in food supply. Another was the greater security provided by the expanded police power of the centralized state. Preventive medicine and extensive improvements in technology, though by no means negligible factors, were not yet developed enough to have the effects that they were to have at a later date. In both periods—before and after 1650—the factor of living space may also have to be taken into account. The European continent, with some few excepted areas, had an abundance of land which could be made to produce sufficient food for its people with the agricultural techniques available. Moreover, Europeans were also moving into sparsely settled overseas regions where their skills could be utilized for the production of wealth and subsistence even more successfully.

As we noticed earlier, however, mere population growth alone is no proof of the success of a civilization in terms of what it can offer to its peoples. The great advantage that western man was to have as his numbers grew after 1650 lay in his ability, first, to create new scientific ideas and technological skills which, in turn, enabled him to exploit previously unused natural resources; and, second, in his ability to use his superior military and technological power to conquer and settle vast overseas areas. As a result, population growth had a stimulating effect because it did not overtax the natural resources or outstrip man's ability to exploit them. Had he lacked these abilities, the lot of western man might have been that of his fellow humans in countries like China or India where population increase, at least prior to our own time, was not accompanied by a general rise in the standard of living. As it was, however, the western world in 1700 stood on the verge of a period of growth during which both population and the level of general subsistence rose simultaneously.

b.   Rise of Cities and Towns (Increasing Urbanization)

The rise of towns and cities was another one of the important characteristics of the general expansion of Europe that began about the year 1000. City origins, like the origins of the expansionist movement as a whole, are somewhat obscure, but it is generally conceded that a revival of trade was the most important cause of the revival of urban life in the West. Not all cities, however, came into existence for commercial reasons. Some, as in Italy, were Roman survivals. Others, particularly in the north of Europe, grew up around fortresses, cathedrals, or abbeys which were important centers of regional administration. In the long run, however, even these were sustained and augmented by trade.

The effects of urban growth on western civilization have been so many and so diverse that it is difficult to summarize them. Some historians have gone so far as to suggest that the influence of urbanization has been more important than any other. Though the point may be argued, there is no doubt that the spread of vast centers of urban population has changed the living habits and even the ideas of modern man in many significant ways.

In the year 1700, however, European towns and cities had not yet achieved the preponderance of numbers and wealth that they possess in our own time. At the opening of the 18th century, it is believed, only two cities in all Europe—London and Paris—had populations of 500,000 or more and thus approached in size and in the complexity of their problems the cities of the 20th century. In almost every state of Europe agriculture was the most important economic activity and commanded the efforts and attention of by far the largest part of the population.

One of the major reasons why city life had not yet become as important or as concentrated as it was to become later was that industrial production was still widely scattered in small handicraft units under what is known variously as the cottage, domestic, and "putting out" system. Individuals and families working in their own homes had no need to live in cities as they would later after the centralized factory came into existence. Most towns and cities, though not all, were commercial rather than manufacturing centers. Furthermore, many inhabitants of cities, right down through the 17th century, tilled their fields during the day and lived inside city walls only at night.

As a consequence, the European way of life in 1700 was still overwhelmingly rural. This did not mean, however, that society had not changed very radically in the centuries since 1000. The rise of towns had transformed the economic and social relations of European society in many ways. Since the very existence of populated centers requires that the agricultural system produce a surplus which can be used to feed those elements in the urban population who do not produce food for themselves, there were created throughout western Europe market areas where the rural inhabitants had changed their agricultural techniques to conform to the needs of the towns. In so doing, the rural producer also changed the system of feudal-manorial relations. Serfs, as they accumulated a surplus of money, were able to transform (commute) their manorial obligations into money payments and often to purchase their freedom from serfdom. Though the processes by which this change took place differed in rate from country to country (in some parts of Europe it was not completed until the 19th century), by the year 1700 the restrictive system of manorial relations had markedly declined.

The growth of cities also had other important general effects. The commercial activities of the townsmen forced them to live outside the customary arrangements of feudal society. Trade required freedom of movement, a different conception of property rights, and a system of law opposed to that of the manor. By striving to win these the town dweller broadened the area of individual action and thus, indirectly, helped to expand intellectual and political freedom. And, finally, the new wealth of the towns eased the rigidity of the feudal class structure and created a new social mobility by making it possible for men to rise more easily in the social scale.

This last development brought into existence a new group within the European social order, sometimes called the burgesses, the bourgeoisie, or, more loosely, "the middle classes." The immediate political importance of this new social element has often been exaggerated by historians, but there is no doubt that these men and the commercial form of wealth they represented did have significant long-range effects on European historical development. By 1700 they were a well-established part of the European scene, and their ideas and influence were to be felt increasingly during the 250 years that followed.

c. Colonization in Europe and Overseas

Though we usually associate migration and colonization with European overseas expansion, Europeans had actually been migrating and colonizing within Europe itself long before Columbus's discovery. From the 10th through the 16th centuries there was a steady movement outward from the more heavily populated regions of Europe into sparsely settled underdeveloped border regions or into areas occupied by non-Christians. Two of these expansionist efforts, namely, the Christian crusades against the Saracens in the Middle East and the conquest of the Greek empire of Byzantium in the 13th century, ended ultimately in failure, but elsewhere Europeans were more successful. Beginning in the 12th century Englishmen undertook the conquest of Ireland, Scotland, and Wales—the "Celtic fringes" of the British Isles. By the end of the middle ages they had overcome the Welsh, partially conquered the Irish, and failed in their efforts to subdue the Scots. In Spain the Christian kingdoms gradually pushed back the earlier Moslem conquerors until in 1491 the last independent Islamic state (Cordova) fell to Ferdinand and Isabella. Farther east, German settlers from the 10th century onward passed over the Elbe and Oder rivers to conquer and Christianize the pagan Slavs of the Baltic region. As the centralized power of the various European states increased, all the peripheral regions were forced to acknowledge the sovereignty of the new nation-states.

Far more dramatic and of more obvious significance in terms of world history was the expansion of Europe overseas. Never again until—and if—space travel becomes possible will men have the same experience that Europeans, beginning with Columbus, had in the 200 years after the discovery of the western hemisphere. Even more remarkable than the fact of discovery, however, were the mass migrations that led to permanent settlement and the transference of European ways and traditions to regions far removed from Europe itself. No movement on such a scale had ever been undertaken in all the world's history. Some notion of the magnitude of this migration may be had if we remember that in the period between 1607, when the first permanent English settlement in North America was made at Jamestown, and 1776, when the American Revolution began, the population of British North America increased, largely by immigration, from about 100 persons to an estimated 2.5 million. What was true of England's colonies was also true, though to a lesser extent, of the colonies of other European powers.

d. The Revolution in the Techniques of Production and Transportation

While it is true that the most spectacular industrial advances of modern times were made from the latter part of the 18th century onward, we now know that for some centuries before that time numerous changes had been taking place in European economic life which made the later development far less revolutionary than has sometimes been thought. Even so early as the 13th and 14th centuries Europe had developed specialized productive skills, most notably in textiles, which had begun to shift the balance of trade with the orient in Europe's favor. In short, European products of all kinds came to be in greater demand; as a result, Europe began to sell more abroad than was imported, a transformation which helped to increase the accumulation of capital (see below). By the 16th and 17th centuries a slow but steady improvement in the technology of production brought on an early "industrial revolution", particularly in the north of Europe. Between 1540 and 1640 the English— followed by the Dutch and Swedes—enormously increased their production of textiles by expanding the "putting out" or domestic system of household manufacture and at the same time accomplished a revolution in the use of coal and iron. There is also evidence which indicates that by the middle of the 17th century England and Sweden between them produced nearly as much iron as all the rest of Europe together despite the fact that the combined population of the two countries was only about 8 million.

More immediately significant for overseas expansion and commerce, however, were the improvements in navigational skill and shipbuilding technology to which every maritime nation of Europe contributed from the 15th century onward. The compass, the rudder, the astrolabe, the true chart made it possible for European ships to sail more quickly and precisely from one point on the globe to another. Improvement in shipbuilding made it possible to transport larger numbers of men and goods in relative safety. What was most important, however, was that in the process navigators and mariners made use of a generalized intellectual skill inherent in the whole long tradition of European thought. The first to do so successfully were the Portuguese and Spaniards. When Prince Henry the Navigator (1394-1460) ordered his ship captains to keep exact logbooks of information gained from their voyages and to contribute that information to a common pool of knowledge, he was demonstrating a European quality which no other society possessed to quite the same degree. Prince Henry was making use of accumulated practical knowledge in a rationalized way for the benefit of the inexperienced and in behalf of later generations. The increase and continuity of such knowledge helped to give Europeans a means of discovery and, later, of colonization far beyond anything known in previous societies. With this development, large-scale transplantation of human beings from Europe to the most distant parts of the earth became possible. One other element was needed to make it feasible. That element, which was capital wealth, we need now to examine in its turn.

e.   The Growth of Capital Wealth

In any society, economic expansion (i.e., the growth of total economic production which alone can raise living standards), while it depends upon a number of factors, cannot occur unless that society possesses two fundamental things. First, it must have a large body of skilled manpower. And, second, it must have an accumulation of what we call "capital." The word "capital" has been given many meanings, but in precise economic terms it is commonly defined as "produced wealth used productively for gain." In this sense, capital is always distinguished from commodities like food, clothes, automobiles, or houses, which, though they have an economic value and may be necessary for an individual's well-being, are not always used directly to produce more wealth. Capital in its simplest form is thus an accumulation of what we call "savings," which are left over from income after all other needs have been satisfied and which may be employed for gainful purposes. For most people the easiest and most obvious way of employing such capital savings is to put them in a bank where they will draw interest. Before savings can earn interest, however, the bank's directors must make use of them in productive ways by investing them in business enterprises or in loans. In this respect, the banker acts as a manager of his depositors' money; and the individual saver is freed of the responsibility for looking after his capital himself. Since banks, in most cases, are fairly safe places to put capital, the interest rate on that capital in return for safety is always relatively low. For those who hope for a larger return, which often calls for a certain amount of speculative risk, the stock market offers another area of capital investment. There individuals keep a somewhat more direct control over their savings by purchasing stocks (capital shares which entitle those who buy them to shares of a company's earnings if profits permit) or bonds (certificates of indebtedness on which interest is paid and which are secured by a company's tangible assets). And, finally, there is a third and much more direct way of employing capital savings. That is by using them to start a business venture of one's own.

All of these methods—and many more—are so much a part of western man's economic experience that he seldom thinks about their historic significance. Often he simply assumes that they are a result of the natural order of things and that they must inevitably appear in any society where wealth has increased to a certain point. Unfortunately, as the experience of many 20th-century underdeveloped societies indicates, such an evolution is by no means automatic. In many instances it is the result of a complex of social factors that almost no societies outside the area of western civilization have possessed to a significant degree.

The first of these factors is surplus product; the accumulation of capital saving, whether undertaken by individuals as it is in western democratic countries or by the state as it is in countries like the Soviet Union, requires that a society not use all of its income for immediate consumption. In other words, its people cannot be living at a level of bare subsistence but must produce a surplus over and above their ordinary needs. Where the level of productive technique is too low or where natural resources are insufficient, the lack of surplus becomes a difficult problem which can be solved only by borrowing capital from some outside source or by further depressing the living standards of society until a surplus is created.

The accumulation of surplus, however, is only the first step in the process of economic expansion. Opportunity to use the surplus productively is a second social factor. A method or methods for deciding what use is a third. In collectivist societies where the state, in effect, controls all economic surplus it also determines how that surplus will be used. Throughout most of the western world, however, the decision as to how savings will be employed has been left up to the individual. Wherever this latter course has been followed certain other things then have to happen if the productive capacity of society is to be expanded by capital investment. Of primary importance to the individual investor is the security of his savings—a fourth social factor. Even when he speculates by putting his money into a new venture he likes to feel that his chances of getting a return on it are at least reasonably good, apart from ordinary economic mischance. He must accordingly have faith in the political and social stability of the society in which he lives—or invests. If the state is in danger of overthrow or if external invasion threatens or if the head of state can seize his money for capricious reasons, then he is likely to keep his money at home in a strong box under the bed. Furthermore, there must also exist a means whereby investor and entrepreneur can be brought together. In the western world this means has been supplied by banks, brokerage houses, and stock exchanges, all of which are devices evolved over a long period of time for the easier circulation of capital. And, finally, one other thing is also needed. Not only must speculative investors have a sense of confidence in their society but they must be willing to forgo immediate economic gains in the expectation of greater ones at some future time.

By the year 1700 most of these conditions existed in a number of western European states but particularly in England and Holland. To a large extent these conditions were the culmination of a process commonly described as the "commercial revolution" by which the capital wealth of Europeans had greatly increased from the 12th century onward. This "revolution" was the result of several causes. One was improvement in agricultural techniques coupled with the rise of towns (whose needs had prompted the rural areas to increase food production above the level of subsistence), which had helped to create productive surpluses in agriculture. Second, the growing power of the state, especially in the national monarchies, provided a stable social and political setting in which men could have confidence that their economic plans had a reasonable chance of coming to fruition. And, third, the development of improved business practices and organization as well as the growth of banks and stock exchanges had twofold effect. On the one hand, an organizational innovation like the limited-liability joint-stock company, by sharing out the risk of loss among many stockholders, greatly reduced the danger of sudden bankruptcy and thus made a greater number of people more willing to participate in large-scale ventures. At the same time, the rise of banks and exchanges made it easier to mobilize large amounts of capital at lower rates of interest which, in turn, made possible the expansion of mercantile and industrial operations. So significant was this last development that some economic historians now believe it to have been almost as important a factor in causing the later industrial revolution as the invention of the steam engine.

In summing up, there are three important effects of this growth of capital wealth that we need to keep in mind. (1) With the creation and circulation of capital the western world hit upon a method of continuously expanding production and, in so doing, made it possible for a larger number of human beings than ever before to enjoy economic benefits formerly reserved for the very few. (2) Because this wealth existed side by side with an improved technology, Europeans were able to undertake overseas colonization and settlement on an unprecedented scale. And (3) the investment of wealth in all parts of the earth during the 18th and 19th centuries gave to western Europe an economic as well as political power that reached around the world.

4. The Problem of Power: the Emergence of the Mass-Oriented State as the Political Form of Western Civilization

In many ways the problem of the state and its authority is the most difficult and permanent with which man has to deal. Despite the confident claims of liberalism, democracy, socialism, fascism, or communism, it seems doubtful that any perfect state, i.e., one that perfectly satisfies all of its citizens, will ever be created. As human circumstances alter, so too must the goals and functions of the state, with consequences that are seldom happy for all groups and conditions of men.

In a general way it may be said that the functions of the state depend upon two things: first, whether it exists to serve the welfare of the few or that of the many; and, second, whether it shall be controlled—even when it attempts to serve the interests of most of its citizens—by the few or by the many. For well over a century western man has tended to assume—though there is still some disagreement on the subject—that the state must serve the interests of all or of a majority of its citizens and that they, in the ultimate, must have a final control over its decisions. The matter cannot rest, however, on these assumptions and practices of the representative democracy, for they are not of themselves sufficient to solve the problems of the state. Even in democratic societies there must remain—and this fact becomes more evident as human problems grow more complex—a distinction between governors and governed, between those who actually run the state and make its decisions and those who only approve or disapprove of that which has been done or decided.

Moreover, the state has always been confronted with a seldom resolved dilemma. The act of governing frequently requires an expert knowledge beyond that usually possessed by ordinary men and a willingness on the part of rulers to make decisions that are necessary for the welfare of all but are extremely unpalatable to an important minority or sometimes even a majority of those who compose the political community. Implicit in this dilemma is the problem of power:

1. In whose interests is the power of the state exercised?
2. By whom is the power of the state exercised?
3. Are there limits, or no limits, to the power of the state? What limits, if there are any, are formed out of ethics? Out of expediency?

By the year 1700 this problem had been temporarily resolved in most western European states with the triumph of the highly centralized absolute monarchy over most other forms of government. England and Holland, however, were two important exceptions. In both of those countries political authority, though far from democratized, was not concentrated in the hands of a king or a royal bureaucracy but was more broadly diffused among the politically significant propertied groups represented in the legislative bodies of those two states. In spite of these exceptions, monarchy was the commonly accepted European form of government and would remain so for more than 200 years. Even in England, where the right of parliament to limit the king's powers in certain areas had been established by the "Glorious Revolution" of 1688, the king still wielded very broad powers and possessed an influence that made him a great deal more than a figurehead.

At this point it is well for us to remember an important historical fact about monarchical government. For centuries it was not only the most widely accepted but the most durable European method of rule. Now that it has almost disappeared we often tend to think of it as having always been arbitrary or unpopular and to assume that those who lived under it were only waiting for an opportune moment to revolt against its authority. Such a belief, while true to some degree of European political attitudes during the last few generations, is not valid as it applies to long periods of earlier history. For the fact is that monarchs and monarchy were not always unpopular. The strong monarchies that came into existence during the 15th and 16th centuries gave to many European societies a security and stability unknown during the middle ages. The king's law and the king's justice, though often imperfectly executed, still provided a greater measure of equality before the law than did feudal courts or customs. The kingly office, too, was a tangible symbol of national power and prestige to an extent seldom achieved by less glamorous elective parliaments or heads of state. But above all else the national monarchies of the early modern period established the practices and patterns of government organization that are still used in democratic states. Modern democracy has retained these while taking over the state and broadening its functions. The state itself, as an institution with clearly defined functions and obligations, was created long before.

Indeed, if we ponder the matter carefully, we can see that without the preparatory spadework of western European kings from the 15th through the 18th centuries, the modern mass-oriented state could never have come into existence at all. What these kings did over several centuries was to institutionalize their office until it became the vast public corporation we now know as the "state." The process by which they attained this end was often slow and twisted; and they themselves had no clear idea of the goal toward which they were working. If they had, they might have rejected it. In most instances, though they had a vague sense of public responsibility, European kings from the late middle ages onward strove toward immediate day-to-day objectives, that is, they were trying to expand their authority at the expense of church and nobles or to convert the uncertain irregular revenues that came to them as feudal overlords of the realm into the regular stipulated payments that we know as taxes. The best evidence of their success may be seen in the gradual transformation of the royal household into a kind of crude state bureaucracy or civil service. At first, most feudal kings were, in theory at least, simply the chief landlords of the realm, though, in practice, they were more or less than that depending on circumstances and the personal abilities of the individual ruler. As they began slowly to expand their powers they also necessarily expanded the functions of their personal servants who made up the royal household. Men who had been the king's personal retainers in time found their responsibilities and obligations enlarged as the king extended his authority over feudal society. As the obligations of his servants increased, the king created other offices and institutions to handle the greater volume of royal business. Inevitably, out of this pragmatic growth there developed a body of institutions with their own customs and procedures. Once this stage was reached— and it was attained at different times in different countries—the king no longer ruled his kingdom as a person but as a kind of corporate entity. He had become a symbol of the state.

Even as the national monarchy reached the height of its power during the 17th century, however, the very proliferation of its services and obligations created new and more complicated problems. With the growth of wealth and social mobility men were less willing to submit to the complete regulations by the state of all standards, beliefs, or social practices. And while many enjoyed the benefits conferred by a strong central authority, they looked upon it with some suspicion and not infrequently resisted its decrees. Furthermore, the property-owning classes often had a strong aversion to meeting the state's demands for the additional revenues needed to keep the state functioning properly. Here we must not forget that most kings did not themselves understand how to resolve this difficulty. Taxation as we know it had not yet come into existence, and most European monarchs even so late as the 17th century still had to depend on their own private estates for a substantial but often hopelessly inadequate part of the income needed to keep the machinery of government in working order. Nor was there anything like a modern funded or national debt which, by providing for regular repayment of loans made to the state, would have kept the state's credit clean. Most monarchs, therefore, lived a hand-to-mouth existence, always on the verge of bankruptcy and often without money for the most necessary purposes. In their struggle to keep solvent, western European kings were caught in a double squeeze. Not only had the costs of government risen as a result of expanded state functions, but they had also been driven upward by a long process of inflation known as the "price revolution" which had been going on since the 16th century. Lacking a modern system of finance, the state staggered from crisis to crisis until some adequate means was found to make up its deficits or, as with England in the 17th and France in the 18th century, the disaster of revolution overtook it.

Nevertheless, the new national or absolute monarchy, for all of its difficulties, not only established the pattern of later government but also provided a relatively secure, if not always equable, environment for the expansion of European civilization. In that respect the modern state is another one of the important inventions of western man without which his history would have been very different.